FROM HERE TO THERE

My Life Story

Edward R. Leon Hamner Sr.

CONTENTS

From there to here

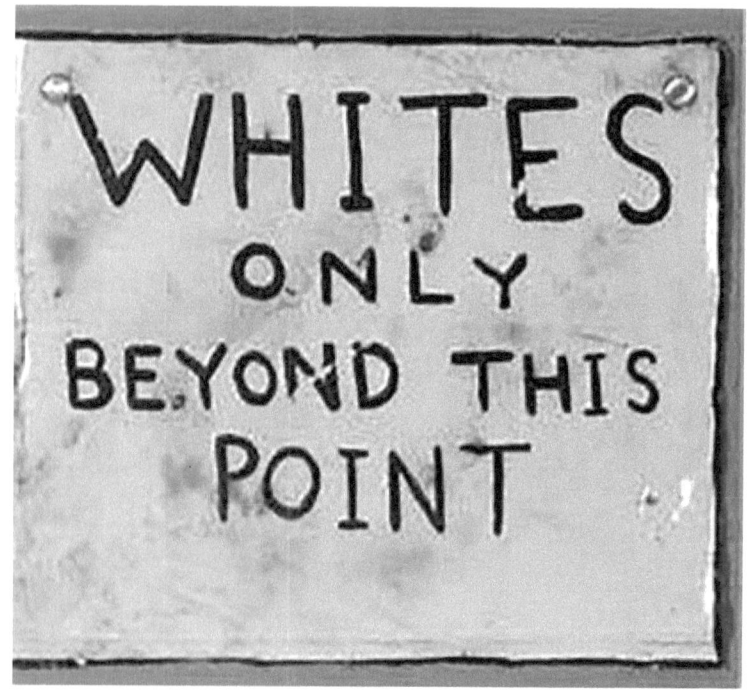

From there

The story you are about to read is a true story with pictures so you can feel the reality by seeing how it was during the Jim Crow era in Peterson, Tuscaloosa County, Alabama.

To here

Preface

This book is written for educational purposes, showing the history of Black people living in the South during the Jim Crow era. This book is about where I was raised and the way I live today in the United States of America. This book should be helpful for many people who are trying to

build a better race relationship in our great country of America. I want to thank all of those who understand and are trying to better educate our citizens on Black history. This book is as accurate in reporting and interpreting the story of my life as I remember it growing up in West Central Alabama during my childhood years though my late teens and from my late teens until today. This book is in memory of the late Rev. H. A. Hamner Sr. and Mrs. Mary Lou Gunn Hamner, my parents who were two great i

Introduction

I am Rev. Edward Rudy Leon Hamner Sr., the son of the late Rev. Henry Allen Hamner and Mary Lou Gunn-Hamner. I was born in Cottondale (Tuscaloosa), Alabama. I was raised in Peterson, Alabama, ten miles north of Cottondale on route 216. My parents were farmers and coal miners. I was born a twin, but my twin brother was born stillborn (dead). I was named Edward Reedy Hamner after Mr. Reedy, the owner of the farm where my parents were living. In 1944, my mother appended Leon to my name. I never knew why I was named after the farmer by his wife, who was the midwife. This book will give information from my birth to the present, 2020. While reading this book, keep in mind that the story that you are reading is true and written in my own words without being edited.

A map of Cottondale, Alabama, to

I want to talk about the law that I was raised under, the Jim Crow law, before I tell my story so you can understand what I am writing about. I will explain the Jim Crow law and how it affected me on my journey in life.

Jim Crow laws were state and local statutes that legalized racial segregation. Enacted after the Civil War, the l aw denied opportunities to Black citizens. These laws were enforced until 1965. Black people could not shake a White man's hand, could not light a cigarette for a White woman or speak to her, and were not allowed to walk near a White woman. Black people could not show any affection toward another Black person in public. We could not hold hands, kiss, or hug another Black person outside of our home. So now you know why Blacks still act that way, because it is the way we were raised. Children never saw our parents kiss or hug. We had to appear like we disliked each other around White people, so we called each other *niggers* just like the White people did. White ministers taught that Black people were cursed by God and were part- animal and that God supported racism and racial segregation, so Whites believed in these ministers. There was also: The way it was was a hard journey that I had to travel, sometimes crying, with my heart aching and pain, but I kept on walking, afraid so many times. I kept walking the road of life. I got very hurt, but I kept walking. I had a vision in mind, so I walked on, stumbling along the way, just kept walking, hungry a lot of times, but

I had to walk on because I had a journey that I had to finish. There were times I wanted to give up, but I couldn't. I traveled on, suffering as I walked. Sometime I wished I wasn't born, but I walked on. I was segregated all along this journey because of the color of my skin, but through it all, I kept walking by faith. I remember what my mother taught us, and that is that there is a brighter day ahead. I prayed day and night asking the Lord God Almighty to help me, and he did. He made my burden lighter. I still remember how I was falsely accused along this journey, but that didn't stop me. You see, the journey that I was on had obstacles on every side, and most of them came from those who hated me because of the color of my skin. It didn't stop me, but it slowed me down so many times. If you live in Southern United States during the Jim Crow days, then you would know that a black citizen at that time were not considered a citizen; we were called part animal and a curse and that God supported segregation and racism; therefore, I had to keep moving on my journey, looking for that brighter day in my life. The life that I had to live as lawless for black people. Not all White people hated us, but the ones who did could do whatever they wanted to do to us, and there was no law to stop them from whipping, hanging, and raping black women and working us without pay, so you see why this journey that I was traveling was so hard to bear, but I kept walking it. Growing up the way I had to grow up was beyond cruel; it was madness with hate attached to it. Now that we learn something about Jim Crow law and lifestyle, it is time to take you through it with me with print and pictures.

Jumping Jim Crow

Jump Jim Crow was when White men would paint their face black and perform jumping like they were dancing like Black people they were playing the blues music, also gospel music.

The Story of My Life

My grandfather who lived with us was born a slave in the State of Virginia in 1845. My grandmother, his wife, was a Cherokee Indian. The Hamners bought their freedom from slavery, but the Gunns, my mother's family, were runaway slaves who changed their name to Gunn.

My parents moved to Peterson, Alabama, when I was two years old, and there is where this story began. Today it is still known as the Hamner Hill. My parents built a log cabin house with two large rooms plus a kitchen. At that time, they had six children to raise and live in that home. When I was five years old, they built another house with more rooms, and my grandfather lived in the log cabin. However, the house was not finished when winter arrived, and they would hang sheets in the ceiling to keep the cold weather out. Our house had a fireplace, potbelly heaters, and a stove in the kitchen. There was no running water, just a spring down the hill that we got drinking water from and a creek to get water for other uses. The house was built from leftover slab from the saw mill where my cousin John Harris worked. The loggers would leave unwanted trees and logs laying in the woods, and my parents used this to build the house with cousin John, and his family lived on the Hamner Hill. We had to bring up that hill every day to supply use and the chicken, hogs, plus other animals that we had. There were fifty-five-gallon drums sitting around the house to catch rainwater. There was a fire under a big black pot with water in it that sit in our yard. This was how they kept hot water for the family to use for washing cloth, bathing, and any needed use around the home. We had no address, no streets, no paved roads, just a dirt or gravel road.

There was no electricity in our community. We used coal oil lamps and candles for lights in our home.

Where I lived at in Peterson, there were no telephones. We had batteries, radio, and windup record players. We played in the woods and swam in the creek, got up every morning early to feed the chicken, hogs, and goats that we had. Weekends, we would walk thou the went fishing in the creek and the river. While walking, we often saw lots of snakes, black snakes, rattlesnakes, and other types of snakes. Also wild animals in the woods. Our father would take us hunting sometimes; however, we went bird hunting daily. Back to our house—it had no glass windows but shutters that we latch at night. There were times that we found and killed snakes in the house. We had lots of cats and dogs around. The floor in the front room was hard dirt floor, and we kept it clean. We always had a piano, a large room with furniture. On Sunday, we went to church. After service was playtime with other children. In those days, the adults in the community helped raise each other's children. They would punish them like their own child, and your parents would punish you also. This really made a difference in how children behave in life and respect older people. My father's motto was always "Who knows the value of a child." We never thought about becoming wealthy. We believed that life would always be like we knew it growing up in the Jim Crow era. Most of our life was living according to the way White people said we should live. We were very poor, poorer than those who live in the ghetto. now days two small stores to shop at no legal service; no law, just the KKK; no doctors; no type of business within ten miles, which we saw about twice a year. If you got sick, you had to depend on your family member to be your doctor and the grace of god for help. Our life was like that of ants, working every day without a leader. We worked to survive, not to gain anything better in life. We knew about electricity but never expected to have any in our home. We knew about running water but never expected to have any in our home. We also knew about telephone but never believed we would have one in our home. The animals we cared for had more freedom than we had. We had a curfew every evening h from the earth because we didn't have any way to survive but to depend on White people who just needed Black people to do their work. This is the way it was as I can remember. The words that I speak are words of hatred but true words about the way it was growing up as a child in my lifetime. There were two words we understand from a up. They are 1) god and 2) nigger. Our whole lives were controlled by these two words. We were taught from birth to serve and obey god and to obey a White person when you are called a nigger. Our parents made do with what they had and lived believing in god Almighty who helped them always. There was no bank to save in. If you had any to save, the only transportation was your foot or mule and wagon. Yesteryears were frightful and a dangerous lifestyle for Black people. Maybe that is why we have high blood pressure, because of the way we were treated by our White brothers. We would wake up in fear every day during the Jim Crow era. Think about how many years Black parents had to raise their children under these conditions without much of anything that a human needs to live on in this world.

Shopping

When going to shop for grocery, we had to walk about one mile to the store. The store was owned by the Body family. This is the family that our family worked for. This the only time we could walk in the White community. At night, we could not walk across the railroad. I will talk about this later in this story. Along route 216, the highway that came through our village there in Peterson, you could find farmers with products sitting up along the road to sell. When we bought from them, we had to pay twice as much as White people. We also had to have our own bags to put the items that we bought in. Sometimes, when our father was ht he would bring the mule we own with a sled to carry back grocery and wood. Lots of time when we children went with them, we would meet White men that would try to take our grocery away from us. We would scream as loud as we can while running so our parents would hear us, our dogs would come barking, and we would then throw rocks at these men also. There were times that these White men would try to make us perform oral sex on them, and if young girls were with us, they would try to rape them. There was no law against a White man raping a Black woman. There was no law officer within twelve miles of Peterson, and we had no phone services or transportation to get to town except by the Greyhound bus that came though Peterson at eight in the morning to noon and six in the evening. You had to walk, or ride a mule and wagon if your family had a mule. There were three Black families in our community who owned a car. My family was one of them. We owned a mule, our cousin owned a mule, and Mr. Tom Scott owned a mule. We didn't have the grocery stores to shop at like city people, so we bought and ate the same type of food over and over again. We had lots of canned food we could buy, plus meats and garden food. There was even a can of beans named nigger beans. Once at the store, you had to wait until all White people were waited on, sometimes standing there if it was raining. Some stores only let Black people shop on a certain day of the week. As far as meat is concerned, we would get the old rank meat sometimes and pay twice as much for it that White people paid for fresh meat. We didn't shop just for the family. We shopped for the livestock that we had also. We had chicken, ducks, hogs, rabbits, and goats.

Shopping for the family was nowhere near like shopping today. We didn't have supermarkets, good restaurants, shopping malls, etc. We only had two local grocery stores in Peterson, Alabama, and they were a mile or more from where we lived. Our parents had a credit account at the Boyd grocery store, which was close to where we lived. We also did work for these people. Both stores would sell rank meat to Black families. There were two supermarkets in Tuscaloosa, which was about twelve miles south of Peterson, and we didn't get to go to town often. We bought fruit and greens from some White local gardeners. We always had chickens in the pen at our home. We shopped in the woods to pick berries and other type of wild food you could find in the woods. Our father went hunting along with other Black men from time to time. Sometimes, our father would take us with him to hunt. We would look for rabbits, l, wild turkey, and other animals that you could eat. We children would go bird hunting with our air rifle. We also went fishing. This is the way we went shopping for the family. Each of these grocery stores had a gas pump so you could buy gas. They were hand-pump gas pumps.

in the black community. If the Black people had not helped one another in the South in those days, we would have vanished by working to death and just buried somewhere in a field. The only way we could get clothing was by mail order. You order them from Sears and Roebuck, National, and J. C. Penney. When they arrived at the post office, the owner would open your package to see what was in them. Now that is what I was told by Mother. This was something done to all Black people receiving a package. There was no other type of shopping for us.

A country grocery store

I sat outside many days waiting for White people to shop before I could go in and shop for my mother, sometimes in the rain; but that was how we Black citizens were treated, so we had to live with it. We had food stamps which were in a book, and you could only use so many each month.

Edward R. Leon Hamner Sr.

Working for a Living

W e worked from home to make a living, and here is how we did it. We went in the woods and picked berries to sell. We sold them for fifty cents a gallon. We, along with Mom, nice Sally and her family, had lots of chicken, rabbits, some hogs, a few cows and ducks. There were lots of peach, apple, plum, and fig trees on our property. We also had gardens. There was a creek at the bottom of the hill on each side of the Hamner Hill, so we sold crawfish from the creek. My mother raised earthworms to sell for fishing. My father did not like to see worms or snakes; he was afraid of them. There were coal mines at the bottom of the hill also, so we got coal from them and picked up coal from the railroad and stored and sold it. My mother was the community midwife and doctor for Peterson and surrounding area. She didn't have a license, but White and Black came to her when they got sick. They nicknamed her "Doctor Yank." She made medication from herbs. Our grandfather built chairs, baskets, and swings and sold them to Black and White people. Our father was a preacher and coal miner. He would sometimes go to work at the mine or church that he pastored in Tuscaloosa, and we would not see him for two weeks. Some of the old boys work on the L&N Railroad. Our older brother went in the army. My mother would take us younger ones in the fields to pick cotton to make money. It was not easy to make a living for a family, so people in the community pitched in and helped one another.

Regardless of how much money you made, it was never enough so you could save any. Looking at the difference in how White people lived and Black people lived is a disgrace to the United States, that they treated Black people this way. There were no standard wages, for as a Black person, you were paid whatever the White man said you was worth for your labor. There was no such thing as eight hours a day; you always work from sunup to sundown. Most Black men didn't have a watch; some could not tell time anyway. Black people worked on the farm, railroad, coal mine, riverboat, sawmills, and other type of work needed with no way of gaining anything in life at that time. But we made it. Everyone in the family worked, parents and children. The large family was what the White farmers wanted. If you had a large family, you would never be without work. You didn't make much money, but you made a living. Working for a living was very hard because we work from sunup to sundown Monday through Friday. Black men worked in the coal mine, sawmill, railroad, warehouse, and on the farm. As a child, I didn't working for a living was very hard because we work from sunup to sundown Monday through Friday. As a child, I didn't understand what Black people was going through to make a living, but as I grew, I started understanding because I had to go to work in the fields at twelve years old. We had chicken and hogs ourselves, so we had to get up early every day to feed them. I watched my father go to work every day. Sometimes he was sick but still went to work. I witnessed Mother work until her hand would bleed working in the cotton field and then go home and do homework, such as cooking for the family and cleaning our home. She was also the area midwife, so she would have to go and deliver a baby sometimes late at night. You notice I show lot of pictures; that is because I want you to see what it looks like working. Seems like you were being punished rather than working on a job. You had to please the boss or get kicked in your behind or whipped with a bullwhip. This was done to adults only. I only worked on two types of job. They are working in the field and working for a family who made pottery and sold it in the market. I helped load and unload the pottery and carried what was bought to the wagon or truck for the buyer. I also worked in a café washing dishes, so when I left Alabama, I had no work skills.

Workers working on the railroad and in the farm

We work with fear every day because we didn't know if the boss was pleased with our work. They didn't whip the little children, but they would whip the adult men and call them *niggers* and made them do a better job. Have I ever seen anyone get whipped? I have seen the White men kick and whip a Black man. There were some Black men who would fight back. My brother was one of them. He would also throw stones and hit them, but the KKK would come looking for him. They would chase my father though the woods but didn't catch him, and he could not come back home, sometimes for a month, and our mother took care of us. These White men would not be mean to our Black women in the area where we lived. This is the way it was from there to here. What a change in life it has been for me when it comes to working for a living.

My mother worked at home raising chickens for a White farmer. She was washing cloth and watching the chickens. My sister also helped our mother. Our father worked in the coal mine, and our brothers worked on the railroad. Our life was to work for White people. That is what we did till 1965 when the rights law was signed.

Living in Peterson, Alabama

Peterson, Alabama, population was about four hundred citizens that included White and Black. There were three grocery stores, the Boyd Grocery, McGee Grocery and U.S. Post Office, and another Boyd Family grocery store. There was electricity in the White community. Some had running water by pumping it in their home from wells. Black people had no running water in their home or electricity, out house for toilets.

There was a school in the Black community. It was for White children only. It was a nice school building. We could not walk across the schoolyard. If a Black person walked across that yard, the KKK would show up, burn a cross, and sometimes whip a Black man and say, "This is a lesson for the rest of you niggers. Do not walk across that schoolyard."

The KKK would come and burn a cross every Friday night so it could be seen by the Black community. Black children had to go to school in the church house New St. Paul Baptist Church from preschool to the fourth grade. The rooms were divided with sheets hanging from the ceiling. A graveyard was in the back of the school alone with two outhouses for toilets. We ate lunch outside under the trees on tables unless it was too cold, then we ate in the basement of the church. The White children had a lunchroom with hot food cooked there by the Black women. Black children had to bring a lunch from home. Sometimes someone would cook a hot lunch for us. My family lived in the woods down a dairy road from the highway. There was another family who lived at the front area of the Hamner Hill, the Gordon Family. There was a path that went from our house to their house. We went into the field to get straw so we could make brooms to sweep our house with, and our mother cut limbs from dogwood trees and made brooms to sweep our yard with. There were always snakes crawling around the yard, some rat snakes, rattlesnakes, and garden snakes. We had lots of dogs and cats who helped us kill them from time to time. We knew how to handle this lifestyle because we were born into it. We knew no other way of life. While walking down the road, if we came upon a White woman or girl, we had to turn our back without looking at them. However, we would take off running like a wild animal. Most White women really would help Black children, but we were afraid of the KKK and took no chance. In 1948, the State of Alabama decided to have the Black children bus to school ten miles to Holt, Alabama, and my father became the first school bus driver to drive a bus for our community. This was the first time a Black child from our community saw the inside of a school bus or a school house. I was twelve years old. The reason we could not walk across that schoolyards was because one man had a club in his home where men and women gather to drink, dance, and also party. One night, two men got in a fight until one killed the other man near that schoolyard. The KKK came and whipped some of the Black men with a bullwhip and burned a cross and said, "We do the killing around here, not you niggers." After that, we could not walk across that schoolyard. The young man who did the killing went to prison for fifteen years. We got up early in the morning and went into the fields to work from sunup to sundown for two to three dollars a day. The men had to work even if they were sick. I saw some Black men whipped with a bullwhip because they were working too slow. It was not a pretty sight to see. They could not fight back because the KKK would come and pull them out of bed at night, tie them to a tree, beat them, burn a cross in their yard, and leave them tied to the tree.

There was only one way in and out of the Black community, and that was through the White community, where you could not go through at night. This was the way it was in Peterson, Alabama, during the Jim Crow era. We were treated like wild animals. Sometimes had to use the thickness of the woods for our toilet. Lots of times, we had no shoes to wear. We would pick up old shoes from trash piles, and Grandpa would repair them for us to wear. We only made it by the grace of God. Just think about using a leaf for toilet paper. Mom would sometimes use feed sacks to make us shirts and short pants to wear. Out of all of this, we made it. We often picked berries to sell. There would be some White men in the woods also. They would see us and say, "Come here, you niggers." We would start running as fast as we could. These men would shoot their guns in our direction, and we could hear them in the tree leaves. Now we don't know if they were shooting at us or shooting to scare us. We were just like wild animals running through the woods from White men. They tried to catch our little sisters and our girlfriends to rape them, and there was no law to stop them. While in the woods, we would find whiskey where they made moonshine whiskey. Tuscaloosa County was a dry county, and you could not sell whiskey. The moonshiners were bootleggers. One of my brothers was a driver to deliver whiskey for them. He had no driver's license. You didn't need a license in the country to drive because there was no law there. If a house caught on fire, it would burn down; there was no fire department. There were coal mines in Peterson, and they went on strike. They would get the Black men along with some White men and bring their guns to work with them because they were going to have to fight the union workers. Of course, we were afraid that our father would get killed, but God blessed him to come home each time they had a strike. These miners were really working for free, because when they got paid, the coal miners' owners also owned the store that they had to shop at. The money was just going back to the owner through the store that they owned. What a way of life. But that was the only way of life that our parents knew about in the Deep South, so they made do with what they had. We went into some of these coal mines to get coal for our home needs. We needed coal for cooking, for fire to keep warm in the winter, also to warm water for baths. Most White people had bottled gas in their home. However, there were some White people who still used coal and wood in their home. Some had electricity. Nature was our pathway of life during the Jim Crow era. My life in the South, in Peterson, Alabama, was not beauty to behold. I wish I could forget it ever happened. I have told you about the coal mine in Peterson, but I didn't tell you that one ran under the Hamner Hill and when the explosions went off.

A Sad Day in Peterson

What made this day sad was while we were playing in the yard, a lady came running and crying and said to my mother, "Mrs. Mae Lou,"— that is what she was called by everyone—"come quickly. The KKK has hung Grover." Mom got up, and went to the community where they had hung him. We found him hanging in a tree upside down. Also, a cross was burning. The KKK was gone. My mother cut him down, and they told her that they had made all the men that were home at the time kneel around the tree and pray. They said that they hung him because he had kissed a White girl. Mom put him on her shoulder and carried him home, which was about a mile away from where they hung him. Now when we got home with him, she discovered that he was not dead. Mom worked on his and he began to grunt and make sounds, so she took some s. Our mother told us not to tell anybody that he was alive. Later that day, one of the deacons from by and told her how they made them sing and pray while they hung him. The deacon didn't know that he was still alive. Mother took care of him until our father came home later that night and saw what happened there, where he could do nothing about it if he had tried; they would have beat him also. The next day, my father went and got some of his mason members and they came with the funeral home van and put him in it as if they were taking him to the funeral home, but they really were taking him to Birmingham, Alabama, and arranged for my mother people to send him to Ohio, which they did. Other Black people in the community didn't know what happened to him, because there was no funeral. If they had known, someone would have told the White people, and they would come looking for my father and mother to harm them. Seeing someone hang in a movie is not like real thing. I will never forget seeing my brother hanging in that tree by a rope. There were other children who saw it also, and that put more fear in us at a young age. We were very afraid of the KKK anyway, but this was different. It was real. We grew up fearing White people and what they would do to us. As we grew older, we had to learn how to survive in life. We couldn't live a joyful life during the Jim Crow era. Some Black people never overcome that lifestyle. They went to their grave fearing White people rather than loving them. That is so sad. This White teenager and my brother did kiss. I understand that they had done it before my brother worked for her family, so somebody told this family what was going on with this girl and my brother. That is how it took place on that Saturday. White people always let a Black man hanging from a tree instill fear in Black people so we would recognize them as being superior to us.

What we saw along the highway sometimes, going to and coming from school. We children had a problem sleeping at night after seeing this. This person hanging in the tree might not have been real, but he looked real to us.

We sometimes saw Black men hanging in trees near the highway on our way to school from the school bus window. A burned cross was always close by, along the road in the field. It might have been fake, to keep us afraid. We live this type of life 365 days a year and knew no other way to live because we were born in this way of life and our parents also. All we could do was dream of another way to live. We knew that lone heaven was a better place; didn't know of anyplace else on earth to live a better life. The little village was quiet that day in the Black and White community. All White people didn't go alone with hanging people. You were not able to get a word out of anyone Black or White. At the post office, the White people would just look at you knowing that you are a Hamner and your family member had been hung.

The White people in Peterson called us niggers at the store. Like always, they talk to us very nice, and that went on for weeks if not months. The White people could not complain because some of the KKK members were in their family.

Meet the Ku Klux Klan. A KKK rally.

This is what we saw as a child and older on the hill just west of the Hamner Hill. They would rally on Friday night and it was frightening. Again, this was not a movie. It was real.

Let Us Talk About the Ku Klux Klan

The KKK was a group of heartless people. Their job was to make sure Black would remain sear gated and to be afraid of White people and to obey them. You had to say "yes, sir" and "yes, ma'am" to their children as well as adults; however, this didn't always work. The Whites would call us *niggers*, and we would call them *crackers* or *peckerwoods*. The only weapon we had to fight back with was rocks, and we were good with rock throwing. The KKK would come in our community just to frighten us. Black did all the work around the White people home, sometimes for a dollar for all-day work. Black women did the cooking, ironing, and house cleaning for a quarter or fifty cents. Every weekend, the KKK came and burned a cross and marched around the area. They would ask, "Is you niggers being good to one another,?" They would ask the women if their husband has been beating them. They would whip a White man for hitting his woman, but they could rape a Black woman with nothing said. The Ku Klux Klan was the law enforcers in the country area and country area. We could not speak to a White woman unless you were a female yourself. Lots of times, it was hard to sleep at night because you didn't know when the KKK would show up. The owner of McGee grocery store was head of the KKK in this area, and we knew it, but we had to live with it. These were some of the dirty people that lived on this God-given earth during the Jim Crow era. They rode on horseback in our community looking for a reason to whip a Black person, mostly Black men. Lots of times, Black men would go in the woods during the day just to not be seen by these KKK members. They treated Black people worse than animals. You better not be caught beating livestock, but it was okay to beat a Black man.

The Ku Klux Klan was treating Black people just as bad as ISIS treat people today in the year 2016. When I watch the news on TV, it brings back memories of my life in the South during the Jim Crow era. I never heard of the KKK burning anyone alive, but they drowned Black people, shot Black people, hang Black people, and drag Black people down the highway behind a truck, also shove them off the back of a moving truck onto the highway. They tied men to a tree and whipped them with a bullwhip. These things happened in Peterson, Alabama, where I lived, and I remember when they did these things. As a young child, I was afraid and asked my mother why they hang Black people. She said they have the devil in them and one day God will get them. Our mother taught us this way. She was a real child of God till she died. These White men whipped Black men as if they were animals, so growing up in life, I had fear of White instilled in my mind. I didn't know any other way to think. Growing up in this part of the USA, I thought I would live like this all my life, working for White people and watching them live happily without any fear. There were some poor White people also and were treated like Black people, but they didn't work in the same field that we worked in. The only time our parents got a break was when it rained and the fields were too soaked with mud. But sharecropping, you still had cattle to take care of, also other animals. I don't just talk about me. I am speaking about Black people, period. When we went to school, other children was talking about the same thing we had to do, so it was the way we lived in the South during the Jim Crow era in life.

None of us had new clothes to wear, but they were clean. Our mothers kept our clothes good and clean.

This was a normal way of life in the Deep South. A Black man didn't have a chance. That is why we complain about police officers killing our young Black men seemingly at will. When you understand what we older Black people lived through, you will see why we will not go back to that lifestyle. We as Black people in the United States of America have come a long way fighting for freedom in our homeland. We help build this country and deserve the same right as any other American. Look at where we come from as a race in this country and willing to forgive all the wrong that was imposed upon us by our White brothers and sisters. The worst thing in our life in the South was the KKK. These were heartless men who hated Black people and had not law to control them because they were the law in the rural area where we lived in Peterson, Alabama.

Father was the school bus driver in Peterson for
Black children in 1948

Getting an Education

When it came to going to school, we had it hard growing up through the years. Black children could not go to school until the crops had been gathered and put in the barns for the winter. Black children in the country and city started school late in the year. We went to school in a church, and some Black children in the city went to school in a barn. White children's school opened on time inside of school buildings with heat in them. We the Hamner family had to walk one mile and a half to that church to school, and there was one teacher who taught all our classes from the first grade through the fifth grade. We walked to that church every Sunday, rain or shine. My first teacher was named Miss Louis, and when she could not come, Mrs. Carrie Lou, our church piano player, taught us. In 1948, when we were bus to school ten to twelve, I attended Holt Junior High School, still no electricity and no running water. Then I went to high school in Northport, Alabama, across the river from Tuscaloosa. We had electric light for lighting. White people made sure that we could not get a good education, or at least they tried. But by the grace of God, we made it. In junior high school, we had to pack our lunch from home. In high school, we could bring our lunch or our parents would pay a weekly amount. We also could go to the store and buy a sandwich. There was a library and study period. We got breaks in between classes. There were playgrounds and things to play on or with, so we did have lots of fun at school. We got a lot of home teaching, although some adults couldn't read or write themselves. My mother was a school teacher when she and Dad got M She taught my father how to read and write. If we could have had, we would have made better grades in school. When we came up North, the school would not accept our grades; they said they were not up-to-date with real grades. The schools up North had lights, heat, playgrounds and ball fields. We studied hard but had to work even as a child before we learned the best that we could. We didn't have very much to learn from. Most books we had in first through the fourth grade in school in Peterson was stories, little reading, some writing, and spelling. We didn't have any school equipment such as chairs or bean. We were in a small church are still there in the same spot today 2016.

We ate lunch under the trees during summer months. That is from April through May. During school lunch breaks, we ate in the church basement during winter. We had one teacher Miss Lewis teaching all classes. She was loved by all of us. We were glad to see her coming. So were our parents.

School classroom in 1945

A school like the one I went to in grade school.
This was also where we went to church.

I never dreamed of going to a school building, but it happened when I went to school in Holt, Alabama, from the fifth through the ninth grade.

Country church house like I went in Peterson, Alabama, as a child, but the KKK burned it down during the sixties, but it was rebuilt and stands there today in that little village. There are a few Black children and grandchildren moving back to Peterson, Alabama. I saw my first marching band, my first football team and game, also my time in a lunchroom of any type at this high school that I went to in Northport, Alabama. The school was Tuscaloosa Country Training High School. In Holt Junior High School, we had mostly used books that came from the White school; however, your parents could go to a bookstore in Tuscaloosa and buy books for twice the price of books for a White child.

In high school, we had new books, electricity, and running water. I had to watch other children to learn how to turn water on to wash my hands. In junior high school, we washed our hands in a wash pan. In high school, we had a sink and water fountain to drink water from. I had a hard time adjusting to this lifestyle, but I made it along with other children who were learning the same thing as I was. There was a cement street that ran to the school also. Now back to junior high school. I will never forget how one of our schoolmates was killed by a White man who shot him between the eyes for playing in a creek behind the school. This man was never brought to court, and in 1995, when I moved back to Tuscaloosa, that man was still alive sitting on his front porch rocking in his rocking chair. My friend was only thirteen years old. This is how they kept us afraid and depending on White people. They did this and never were punished for doing it. We made it through all of these hard times. Thank God he is real and in charge. The shooting of my schoolmate took place in Holt, Alabama, where I went to junior high school. I remember this as if it had happened yesterday. When I see the *Zimmerman v. Martian* case in 2013, I see one step back toward the Jim Crow era. My schoolmate was killed in 1948. We were always afraid while in the woods playing or picking berries because we didn't know when a White man would show up, and they always chase you for some reason are sick a dog at you.

High school building

Home in the Country

L iving in the country was a lifestyle that Black people had to live that was almost worse than animal life was. As a child, we were told to never talk back to a White person and answer with a smile saying "yes, sir" or "yes, ma'am." If you don't obey, they whip you with a bullwhip, so you see, we didn't know any other way to live. It was in our blood system. When you worked for them, you could just expect what pay you got, some a dollar for all- day work. You spent most of the day in the woods and learn the woods life just like city people learn the city. We knew where to go by landmarks in the woods, never getting lost. There was wildlife of all type—wild cats, black bears, deer, and many other types of wild animals, plus plenty of snakes. There was no recreation in our community for children or adults. We had to build what we had from thrown-away scrap found in trash piles in the woods are along the highway. We Black citizens had to build a dam in the creek so we could swim. There was no civilized life for us Blacks in the country. We made do with what we had. There was no doctor, no clinic, there was no hospital or transportation to get to anywhere but by mule and wagon. My mother became the community doctor. There was no place to buy clothing or home needs. You can only go to town if you worked during the week. What things you could buy was limited because you had to bring it back on the Greyhound bus, riding in the back seat or standing. My parents had a small store in our home where Blacks could come and buy things to carry them through the week till weekend. They also had a restaurant in town, but they didn't put all the money in the bank because the bank would keep what Blacks made over what was allowed for a Black to bank.

L&N Railroad came through our community between the Black and White area, and we could not cross that railroad after six o'clock in the evening. The KKK, with the help of other Whites and Black people who we call Uncle Toms, told them everything we Blacks did in our community. Here is how the Ku Klux Klan kept us under control. They kept us afraid at all times without letting up. They would always say, "Come here, nigger," or "darkie." Sometimes they would say, "Come, you crow," always in a mean way, cursing. They KKK would enter our community unexpectedly from time to time. We never knew when they were coming. Just think, all your youth and teenage life you lived this way with fear. I did. They kept us uneducated by not allowing us to get the proper school supplies that were needed in any school. We got used books of their choice from the White school. These books were the ones that they were throwing away. Black teens had to work on the Railroad, coal mine, and highway at age fifteen and up. We always entered school later than White children. In the country, a lot of our clothing had to be passed down from the older children. Our mother patched them up and passed them down. We saved the cow feed sacks, also flower sacks, so Mom would make us clothing from them. White people made sure that we had to depend on them. We never had enough of anything we need but food. They kept us alive so we could take care of them. Blacks work in mills, factories, sawmills, and other types for three dollars a day. We live just like they were during the time that my grandfather told us about when he was a slave. We were born scared of White people, uneducated, and depending on White folks. Sometimes we went to the store for corn meal and we had to buy spoiled meal with bow weavers in it, which is a little bug that got in corn and cotton. Mom used a sifter to get the bugs from the meal. During this time, a loaf of bread cost five cents a loaf. Kool-Aid was one cent a pack.

Walking along the road, you would see where the KKK had burned a cross and left it standing. We understood that they were always somewhere around, and we did what was called staying in our place, meaning don't do anything that a Black person was told not to do. As a child, I saw with my own eyes Black men whipped by White men in the cotton field with a bullwhip because they say they was working too slow. Then we had to pick cotton faster. Sometimes these men were sick, but that didn't matter. I saw my father being chased in the woods like a wild rabbit, and all we could do was say, "Run, Daddy." They didn't catch him because we knew these woods like the back of our hand. You would look up and see another White man coming, with bloodhound dogs to go in the woods looking for him. We knew he had to pick coal for the winter. There was one way in and out of our community, and there was a road sign that said TNT, meaning "Trot, nigger, trot." This was life in the country. About three miles south of Peterson was a grit mill. This is where we took corn to be ground into meal and grits. It was near Hurricane Creek, a creek where we did lots of fishing, also swimming. The Black Warrior River also ran though the west side of Peterson where we went fishing sometimes. I remember a young Black child that we call Red. His family was the Harris family. They let Red go to Tuscaloosa, and while he was in town, he was struck and killed on a bicycle in Alberta City. The White man that hit him with his car was not arrested; he just walked away a free man. That is how it was for Blacks in the South. His family brought him back to Peterson to have his burial. His stepfather was shot by three White men lying in the bushes near their home because he been urging with his wife. He lived, but these White men were never arrested. There are many stories like this in the South during the Jim Crow era. We were always afraid for our fathers and brothers but not our mothers, because White men love our Black women. They would send the Black men to the fields and rape their wives while they were away. The Black women are the ones who saved the Black men's lives in America because of their love for Black women. Black women took care of their home for them. They did the cooking, cleaning, and help with the children.

This is what we saw every day. This was not just this where we played at every day.

We feed chicken, ducks, pigs, and goats. We had fun while feeding them. Most Black families had chicken running around in the yard. We also had a garden that we work in at home.

Children in the family worked in the farm while we lived in the sharecrop farm. We cried sometimes, but we kept working.

Growing up in Peterson, we didn't have a lot of things to do. We played in the woods most of the time. On Sunday, we went walking with our parents after church service, and that was very nice. We had toys to play with that our parents bought when they went to town. We built lots of toys from cans, hard mud, sticks, and corn cobs. We went skinny-dipping in the creek. The men made a playground near the church for us. There was a swing hanging from a tree, seesaw, spinning wheel, slide board, horseshoe games. We played softball in a little field there in the community. We would go bird hunting and fishing from time to time. There was not very much for us to do other than work for the White people. The thing we looked forward to was Christmas. We had a grand time. During Thanksgiving season, we went turkey hunting with our father and killed a turkey most of the time. It was a sad lifestyle growing up as a child because there was nothing like what children in the city had. We loved to go to the river and watch the barge come by with coal in them. Of course, as a child, we did a lot of playing, not knowing what our parents were really going though as Black people. We didn't enjoy life the way it was meant to be because of the color of our skin. We sat along the roadside and counted cars as they passed by. Each one of us would choose a color and see who would have the most cars of their color pass by. It was fun to us. We went in the woods and swung on vines, also hunted birds with our BB guns and homemade bow and arrows. We knew what time the train came though Peterson so we would go and watch the trains go by. That included the passenger train.

Every morning, our parents got up to milk the cows and feed the animals, and our mother would be in the kitchen cooking breakfast. And churning the milk for butter to be sold. We learned how to make butter as children.

All family members went in the field sometimes to pick cotton, pick potatoes in baskets, pick peas, and pull corn. They raised peanuts on this farm plus all types of garden food such as greens, beans, and many other products. There was always a watermelon patch, cabbage, cucumbers, tomatoes, onions, and lots of other vegetables. We helped carried lunch to workers in the field that the hired hands had cooked for them. These men were plowing and planting this sharecrop. We were safe from the KKK as long as we stayed on the farmland. Whites didn't allow the Ku Klux Klan to bother their sharecroppers. Our sister worked at the owner's home. My little brother and I carried water all day to the workers in the field and had fun doing it. At harvest, we helped gather the crop and carried it to the market in Tuscaloosa to be sold. We also sold it along the highway. Black children on the farm had to help with the crop gathering before enrolling to school in September. No White children had to work in the field with Blacks, but the older ones helped with the farm animals. My mother taught us at home until we could enroll in school, but the White people didn't know it. The Boyd family never called us niggers; they called us colored people. Living on a sharecropped land was hard work, but Blacks had to make a living the best way they could or their family would go without food to eat. We didn't have to worry about clothing or food while we sharecropped. We wore overalls most of the time. That is farm clothing supplied by the owner. The dairy farm we lived on was a barn where you milked the cow with our house built on to it. Mom would walk out of the side door right into the barn. We were really living with some of the cows. There was a large swimming area behind where we lived, but we could not go near it. We had electricity and running water plus a bathtub. It was the first time I saw a bathtub or a kitchen sink. Our sharecropping days were about to end because the older children were moving up North, as we called it. They moved to Ohio. Our older brother went in the army. We as children didn't really know what our parents were going through on this farm. There was a lot of livestock, also pigs, cows, mule, and chicken. We children enjoyed living on this farm, but we didn't know how hard it was on our parents. They worked five days a week from sunup to sundown to raise their family. Here are some pictures of what is on a sharecropped land.

Once the truck is loaded, these workers waited for the farm to send someone to carry the truckload of produce to the market. This is the only time that they got rest from the day's work.

This is the type of work that we Black people did every day for a living with little pay, if any at all. Sometimes the farmer gave the workers some of the crops they accomplished that day.

I worked in fields after I was a teenager. The farmer picked us up and carried us to the farm that they owned. The farm was not in Peterson. It was in the North River area, which was about thirty miles from Peterson. On the Colema family farm, my mother gathered the workers for him, and she got paid to do this for this farmer.

This wagon load of cotton was headed to the farmer's barn and stored till it was time to take it to the cotton gin to sell. The cotton gin was a processing plant where cotton was sold to different businesses that made clothing and others.

I never loaded a truck like this, but I saw the men on the farm loading a truck. The cotton had been weighted and placed in a stack.

These are some pictures of the things you find on a sharecropping farm.

What you see is a tired young girl who has worked in the hot sun picking cotton so their family can make enough money to survive on. Working in the cotton field was not easy. I know firsthand about it. I worked hard picking cotton, but our parents kept the money we earned that day, and we knew why they did. We had a piggy bank that our mother put money in for us for our savings. There was nowhere to spend it anyway in Peterson, Alabama.

There were signs in some areas that said TNT. This meant "Trot, nigger, trot." We ran like wild rabbits. There was only one sign like this that I saw in Peterson, Alabama, along route 216, which run through Peterson.

We picked cotton the same way in the 1940s through the 1950s. I saw Black people on their knees picking cotton in Akron, Alabama, in 1997. We still have a long way to go when it comes to reaching true freedom for Black people in the United States of America. We didn't just pick cotton. We had to pull corn, pick peas, pick up sweet potatoes, and take care of the cattle and other farm animals. We had to go to the market and help sell the produce, also set up stands along the road. Remember, my younger brothers have their story because they lived life a little differently because they moved to the city, whereas I didn't get that chance. My older sister and my will have a story of their own. She can talk about things I never saw or told about. Picking cotton in the '40s was same as picking cotton in the eighteen hundreds. You were on your knees all day five days a week from sunup to sundown. We had to do this for a living. There was no other choice.

Barn on a sharecropped farm

Farmers used these barns to store grain and hay for the cattle on the farm, plus seeds to be planted next spring. We bedded sweet potatoes in these barns by burying them in mud and pine straw, and they stayed fresh that way. We would also hang cured meat in the smokehouse. We had an icebox in the kitchen to keep some food cold. These barns had hay for the livestock to eat. They kept feed for the animal. The wagons were kept in these barns also. Plants seeds were also kept in these barns, and everything that was harvested. There were livestock fenced in a pasture also. These barns were a must and had to be kept in good shape; and of course, it was the Black men who did the work.

We are returning to our home in Peterson. This was good news for us children. Back to our playground in the woods and creeks. Our dogs were still there, also our own chickens and ducks. Our parents went back to our home. Our cousin still lived in a house there and kept everything around the house. It was still in good shape. Our house was built with cement blocks. It was the only house in Peterson with a basement, Black or White.

Black Warrior river dam in Peterson, Alabama, in 2020. Mule and wagon is what was used to move our furniture back to Peterson This was the best way to make a living for Black people. One year after the harvest was over, my parents decided to move back to the old homestead. You always moved by mule and wagon, and it took more than one trip unless you own a mule and wagon. The other farmers remained on that farm. We still went to school with them. The little old house was still there with no running water, no electricity, no inside toilet, just an outhouse which was still standing. We were back to carrying water from the spring down the hill from our house. Our cousin Sally and her family plus the Gordon family were still living there, and they were so glad to see us back. We are now in Ku Klux Klan territory, back to cross burning. My parents decided to build another house and build it with cement bricks. It had three bedrooms, living room, dining room, kitchen, a basement with two small rooms, plus a porch. My father was still a pastor in the city of Tuscaloosa. There were some new homes built in the White community and a post office built onto the McGee grocery store. My mother rented a P.O. box, box twenty-six. My family was still working for the Boyd family there in Peterson. We were driven about twenty miles a day to pick cotton up the North River for the Colman family.

This was across the Black Warrior River though Tuscaloosa and Northport, Alabama. We did this for a few years to make a living. Our father was working in the coal mine again and pastored two churches.

This is a picture of Peterson wooded area today, 2020

We enjoyed these woods growing up. Lots of birds to be found. We had chickens and lots of rabbits. Our mother raised them for a company in Tuscaloosa. There was theater built in the White community at this time. Black people could only go there on Tuesday night from six o'clock until eight o'clock in the evening, then return across the railroad. One Tuesday, the Black men were invited to come see a special movie. Once inside, the movie didn't come, and they were told that it was running late getting there. What a surprise. Some White person came in and said, "You got to come outside." When they got outside, to their surprise, a cross was burning and the Ku Klux Klan were everywhere you looked.

They said, "We heard that a Black is having an affair with a White woman and we want him." They were going to hang him that night. No one told them anything although they knew he was. The KKK started whipping them with bullwhips, but they could not get away because they were surrounded by the KKK. These Black men took beatings. My older brother was with these men. They said that they been meeting in the woods and they are going to kill this nigger. We never knew what happened to the White woman. There was a Black man telling them about this woman meeting the Black man. Everybody knew who told it. He was known as an Uncle Tom, afraid to death of White people. They finally let the men go and said, "We will find this nigger and hang him by the neck and hang whoever hid him." Now this man was one of them who had been beaten that night. My oldest sister worked for a White family and would hear them talking about this incident and our mother what was said.

The only freedom we had was at church service. White people respected the house of God. I still can remember going to town with my father. My younger brother was with us also. When we were through shopping, we went to the Greyhound bus station to catch a bus. When the bus was loading, they said to my father, "We don't have room for any niggers," so we started walking. It was five o'clock in the evening. We walked just about three miles, and a White man who my father was a minister stopped and gave us a ride home that night. The KKK was still looking for this Black man; however, White women came into these woods looking for Black men all the time for sex. While the man was away working in the coal mine, these miners came home on the weekend. So did our father; he worked in these mines also. These mines were located about twenty miles north of Peterson, in Brookwood, Alabama, off route 216. There were also script mines along the highway in Fleetwood, Alabama, north of Peterson. There were mines in Peterson. There were two mines under the Hamner Hill.

One day, we got word that the KKK had found this Black man that they were looking for. One Saturday, the KKK came and gathered Black people in the community, including children. They gathered Black people from other areas near Peterson. There is Gilmore, Fleetwood, Suzz, Kelmar, and Brookwood. They lined these people along with White people and said they were going to show a special show. Now this Black man was named Mr. Woodrow, and he liked to play his guitar and sing the blues. He would sing little rhyme songs to children also. The KKK put him on the back of a log truck while he was playing his music, and when he got where crowed, they came riding down route 216 at a high speed and threw Mr. Woodrow onto the road and killed him that way and said, "This is how we treat niggers when they are having relations with White women." The Black community was now very afraid even to sleep at night because they would sometimes wake up from their sleep by a burning cross in their yard, and they had done no wrong. It didn't stop there. One day, young Black men went to the river where a creek merged into the river. That is where they swim at. Some White men came and said, "We know that another nigger have been seeing a White woman in the woods and we come to get him." They knew it was true. Again, these White women always came looking for Blacks for sex and gave them a choice. The choice was, "You will have sex with me or I will scream rape." Now they took this man and drowned him while the others looked on. This man's name was Ike Folly. My brother was there also. He left Alabama and never came back until 1998 when he came to visit me and my. We had moved back there in 1994.

There is one other thing that I want to tell you about the life in Peterson, Alabama, and that is when I was a child, and it still bothers me today trying to figure out the reason Whites could treat a little child the way they did. I am talking about my little sister. She was only two years old. Everyone has a breaking point, but I was a small child, nine years old. Our father was in town that week. He was running a church revival in Tuscaloosa, Alabama. There was no way to contact my father ten miles away. What happened is my little sister became ill, and Mother had to get her to a doctor. With no way to get her there, she had to wait until the next morning to catch the Greyhound bus. My mother and sister stood on the road and flagged the bus down and went to Druid City Hospital in Tuscaloosa. When she got there, the Blacks had to go to the rear of the hospital to enter the hospital. Mother signed in the waiting area about eight thirty in the morning. My mother held her child in her lap while my sister stood in a line, but every time a White person came in, they would not see a Black person. This went on from eight in the morning till four in the evening. My sister and mother took turns holding the child. At four o'clock, a doctor finally came and asked what was wrong with the baby, and she explained it to him and said she is asleep now, so the doctor her and said, "Mrs. Hamner, this baby is not sleep. She is dead." We don't know what time she died; however, my mother had to catch the last bus out of Tuscaloosa to Peterson, so she had to leave little Sally Ann Hamner there until Ford Funeral Home could pick her body up. My father worked for this funeral home during the day while he was in town, so he went and picked our little sister's body up from the hospital. I was nine years old, and when Mom came home, she didn't have our little sister with her. We asked, "Where is Sally Ann?"

She said, "It is bedtime for you children, and I will tell you all tomorrow."

The next day, our mother told us our little sister was gone to heaven, but that didn't work with me and my older brother and sister. I remember saying I am going to kill every White person from now on. We were all crying the next day. Me and my younger brother went in the woods with stick guns, looking at trees, calling them White people; and if I had the chance at that time, I would have really been looking for White people to shoot. It was bad. My mother sat me and my brother down and talked to us. She said, "Look, don't hate anybody, children. Tell God about it." But I couldn't see why they allowed my little sister to sit there and die because of the color of her skin. She said to me, "Son, there will be a change coming one day. Just hold on." I didn't really know what she meant, but I love and believe my mother. Today I am thankful for her advice. She saved my life, because I wanted every White person dead at that time. After I was out of high school, during the summer, I went to work at Elvin Drill in Tuscaloosa for twenty-five cents an hour for eight hours plus weekends. There was a deacon working there who was dating Elvin, who was a White woman who owned the place. The deacon was a Black man, and I was scared to death every day. Mom let me save my money and buy some clothing and other things. My older sister had moved to Cincinnati, Ohio, and Mom sent my younger brother John to live with them so he could get a school in the North. My last summer in high school in 1954, I got my pay from work and went home that night to Peterson. I asked my mother for my savings and caught the Greyhound bus the next day and went to Cincinnati and went in the army. I didn't go back until

1975 for a week, then went back again in 1994 and lived there until 1999. I have told you about from "there" now the rest of the story to "here." Living in Peterson, Alabama, was a lifestyle that I would not want to see any other human have to go through. That is why we as a Black race will not go back to such a lifestyle. Time was hard every day bringing water from under the hill for drinking, washing, bathing, and for the livestock. We carried it in buckets, sometimes half a day to get the supply of water needed. But now I am moving into a new life a long way from home. I had to leave my father, mother, two younger brothers, and an older brother and his wife in Peterson, but my parents moved to the of Tuscaloosa after I had gone away. My parent to Tuscaloosa I never live there as a child live there in 1995–1999

Tuscaloosa, Alabama, 2020. The city is coming back
after the great storm almost destroyed it.

A coal mining area in Alabama, not in Peterson

Coal mining was one of the better ways to earn a living in Alabama. Black and White men worked in these mines. A lot of these mines were just holes on the side of like the mines in Peterson. Miners wok on their back most of the time all day digging coal. Some had donkeys to pull the coal in box cars from the mine to the trucks loading docks.

Black and white men worked together in these mines. White men that worked in the mine were also poor people. Some lived near the Hamner Hill at the road that came from the highway to our house.

The picture shows two scrip mines. They dig in the ground for coal, not go underground for it.

type of coal mines was located in the northside of Peterson. My father and brothers worked in these mines.

These scip mines was located near route 216 and about a mile and a half from the Hamner Hill, and we walked up there to see them work these big machines. We call them steam shovers.

And dig coal there were lot of dump trucks loaded with coal and drove away to the area in Peterson where they loaded the coal on the train box cars. Some of the young Black men work at this loa

Moving from There
Going to Here

In summer 1954, I made my move with my guard brother, went to join the army in Tuscaloosa, Alabama. But they wouldn't let us join. So I went to Ohio and joined the US Army. This is where the story "here" begins. Once in Cincinnati, Ohio, I learned a new lifestyle. No more "yes, sir." I learned what it was to have a bathroom and inside home drink water, and have all types of business and movies to go to. Black people owned beautiful homes, cars, and trucks. They also owned cafés and stores. We could ride in the bus and sit anywhere we wanted to on that bus. There were streets with street cars riding up and down them. Now this was over to much for me. I would just sit up and look at the lights and cars go by late at night. We lived on the third floor in that building, but I had never been in a building that high before. We had no windows to look out of like that in Peterson, Alabama. I would go to downtown Cincinnati and stand and look at the tall buildings. There were all types of stores to shop at, and I had never seen that before. I am now eighteen and learning life all over again. Across the Ohio River in Kentucky, it was the same as in Alabama, so I didn't like to go over there. Living in Cincinnati wasn't that great. At night, you could not go in some area of town after dark. You could not be caught in Norwood, Ohio, just north of Cincinnati if you were a Black person. The same in St. Bernard. We had gangs in the city also, so I joined a gang called the Buzzville Gang. We would have fights with the Vine Street Gang, which was a White gang. They didn't want us to cross Vine Street after dark. There was a place called the Black Beer Lot on Colerain Avenue. They sold bark beer there. The beer was dark black. Now we could not go any further after dark without being stopped by the Cincinnati police. We weren't allowed up in price for nothing but to go to work if you had a job up there. There were lot of parks around, and I went to them during the summer. The Union train station was famous, and people would take their child and lay in the park, sometimes most of the night. Schools were segregated still, but they were very good schools. There were some cafés that Black people didn't go in but hot in the downtown area. After staying there for a short period of time, I decided to go on in the army, and this is where I grew up at, in the military. Now life began here this way. I went to downtown Cincinnati and joined the army but didn't tell anyone that was what I was doing because they would have discharge to do so, but my mind was made up before I came there. After being enlisted, I said that I wanted to leave that day and go to camp. I didn't know what I was doing, but I did it anyway. It was time for me to grow up and go on my own, so I chose the military.

Later that day, I was sent to the processing center in Fort Thomas, Kentucky. There I did lots of paperwork. I also was sworn in by raising my right hand, which was something I had never experienced before. We were not allowed to swear when was coming. We were told that God would punish us. The Bible also taught us not to swear. I only had clothes to wear when I left Alabama, so I caught the Greyhound bus to Cincinnati and went in the army. I was green as grass in life, didn't know anything about manhood, just that I was on my own and away from running from White folks, and that felt good. I didn't see it, but I felt a change was coming. I didn't know what to expect because I had never been on my own before, so I had to learn how to cope with other people. I made it here, but I still had a long way to go to reach what I was looking for in life.

Downtown Cincinnati, Ohio 2

Cincinnati Findlay Market. This has been a famous place to shop for decades. People from all over the USA came to Findlay market. I once lived about three blocks from this market.

Brent Spence Bridge that crosses the Ohio River from Cincinnati to Kentucky. I wasn't here very long before heading to the US Army. I didn't tell anyone that I was leaving. I just drifted away. The next time my family heard from me, I was in the army growing up and learning about real life. I went across this bridge after enlisting in the army. I didn't cross it again for three years after I was released from the US Army.

Life in the Military

Fort Thomas, Kentucky Fort Thomas in 1955

We were now processing all paperwork that was needed to enlist in the army. There we were driven to the military post at Fort Knox, Kentucky. There for the first time, I saw a military post. I had to take a full exam and shots before I could go any farther with this process to be inducted into the army. Fort Thomas was located just across the river from Cincinnati in Kentucky.

This is where my life out of the South began, a lifestyle that I will never forget. I heard about the army, but now I am going to learn first. We gave up these street clothing and into the US Army clothing. They gave us a flying twenty ($20). It bought toiletries and Bugler tobacco, with no change for anything else. You got a haircut, a bath, and clothing from quartermaster at headquarters. We fell out of bed at five o'clock the next morning, had breakfast from six to seven o'clock. We were then showed where we would be staying, known as the barracks. There we met some NCO officers (noncommissioned officers). These were sergeants. We went to classes after that and were told, "You are in the United States Army now. Forget your mother and we are your parents." Knees begin to tremble for we now know what it is going to be like. We were taught how you know the different ranks in the military, also who to salute and who not to salute. We were told our rank and how much we would get paid each month. I was a private second class at $71 a month. We learned where the Post Exchange (PX) was, the clinic, the Lunch Hall and Parade field were located. At five o'clock, we gathered to the flag lowering and salute it while it was coming down. Then we were off for the day. Now lights were out at eleven that night and the sergeant made bed check to make sure everyone was present.

Next day, we fell out of bed and gathered outside. We were taught how to march to the mess hall to eat. We went back in the building after eating to learn how to make our bed up military-style. We had to clean the floors on our knees with a hand brush, sometimes with a toothbrush. You had to take a shower every evening. We was also taught how to hang our clothing and put our clothing and other items in our footlocker that sat at the foot of our bunk bed. The person on top locker was at the foot of their bed and the person on bottom was at the foot of their bed. Now training started. We learned to march and pull guard on post. We started out pulling fireguard with a wooden stick gun walking around the building at night. You walk two hours, then sleep four hours. This went on for a few weeks, then we were told where we were going to get our basic training. Coming from the farm, sharecropped land, and Jim Crow era, I was completely lost. Instead of running from White men, I was equal with them, and they were saying "yes, sir" as loud as I was to other White and Black men in uniform. Just think, I could walk in a room and take a shower and had my own bed. This was a day I never dreamed of. Now life was changing in a way I never knew. I was getting ready to fly in my first airplane. I had watched them lfly by in the air many times. I couldn't believe I was eating in the same kitchen as White men. Didn't come in from the back door. We grew up knowing about the gold in Fort Knox, and here I am in Fort Knox. What a dream come true. I could write and tell my parents that I was in Kentucky where the gold is, but it had not sunk in yet that I was in the army. Once issued my uniforms, I began to feel like I was in the army now. Just think about how I must have felt coming from Jim Crow era to a civilized world. I was told that we would be getting ready for basic training, but not here at Fort Knox. Next day, I got my orders that I would be flying to Fort Riley, Kansas. We were marched to a group of military trucks and loaded into them and headed to the airport. Once there, we were loaded in the airplane. I was scared so bad the soldiers beside me had to calm me down. The two soldiers were from Cincinnati, Ohio. This is where my new life began with new friends, and most of them were White, whom I had been running from all my life up until now. I still had fear of White people. It didn't change overnight. I had been taught all my life until now to fear White people because of what they could do to Black people. As I travelled my journey in life, I had seen other Blacks be abused by them and whipped, kicked, and killed, so I didn't know what to expect out of these White men in the army. I finally learned that life was different here in the military. Black and White were treated the same way and went through the same training together. And now my journey is making a turn for the better so far. I was still walking by faith at this point in life.

I did some training here in Fort Knox. This is where I got my first military uniform. The first time going in a barber shop to get a haircut. This was not what I expected, and I am already missing my mother and father, also my little brothers. I knew I was not going back to Peterson, but I started missing it. I had no problem with getting up early in the morning; I had done this all my life. I learned how to march and work as a team. This was the first time I saw the amount of money I got, $71 a month. I didn't know what to do with it, but the platoon leaders took us to the store and showed us what to buy uilding until I was sent to Fort Riley, Kansas, I was on guard, fire duty recruit with a wooden fake rifle on my shoulder. All newcomers had to pull guard duty like this.

On my way to a new life that will teach me how to protect the country which is the United States of America. After landing in Fort Riley, Kansas.

This was the first time I had seen an airplane and flying in an airplane. Couldn't wait to tell my family about this. All of us were enlisted men so we was fixing to go through the same type of training. We didn't know what to expect, but we would soon find out.

I was now in the Tenth Infantry Division Eighty-fifth Regiment Third Battalion Mike Company Recoilless Rifle Platoon. These heavy weapons, tank killers and bunker buster—I had never heard of any of these before, so I was all eyes. We were fed and assigned to a platoon where you would have a platoon leader plus section leader, first sergeant and platoon leader who was a second lieutenant. These are the ones who I answer to every day while in the name, but today I still wish I had gotten her name because she and I integrated that place in 1955. Now when we went in town, we went to a café where they were serving Black and White soldiers. When we would come out, there were some young White teens that would call out "nigger lovers," but we would just laugh and go about our business. Now in my mind, I was seeing Peterson, Alabama, all over again. Here I am getting ready to go overseas to defend this country but could not eat or drink from the same café as White soldiers. This didn't stop us from going downtown. We needed the freedom from training. Today I still wonder where that bold lady is. May God forever bless her and her family. Did she tell her family about this like I did? By now I had found some Black soldiers to go to town with while on pass in the future what I am fixing to go through is not a dream or nightmare; it is real, with a lot of pain, but I am still walking this journey to reach here?

Tenth Infantry Division. Getting up at five in the morning didn't bother me because I had to get up that time every day growing up to feed the animals. We had chickens. We got up, went to chow—that is, to eat—at six o'clock, and start training at eight o'clock. It was always hurry, hurry, hurry. We were taught how to march and how to clean our boots and shoes. After the first week the ral training, we were issued a weapon that we would carry. My weapon was an M1 rifle. I learned everything about this weapon. I could put it back together blindfolded, then I was told that I had to sleep with the weapon and take care of it, which I did. I was then t another weapon, the carbine. I had to learn everything about this weapon also. During this time, we were also running in formation on the parade grounds. First thing in the morning, we had to go on police call—that is, pick up all trash on the grounds where we live, which is the barracks, then other assigned areas. At five thirty in the evening, we went off and took a shower, then we could go to the PX, movie, or club that was on post. We could not leave the post on a pass because we were still in basic training. You could not drink any alcohol until you were twenty-one years old. I didn't drink or smoke at that time although you were issued a pack of Bugler tobacco. Every morning, they would inspect your bed to see if it was made up correctly, inspect the way your clothing was hanging to see if your shoes and boots were clean and shiny. The sergeant made sure that your clothes were clean and buttoned right. Everybody had to have their clothing alike, or you had to do it until you look alike in uniform. After eating, you had to start exercising—that is, push-ups. There was a certain amount of push-ups that you had to be able to do. I can't name all the exercises that we had to do. Each day, there was different type of training that you did. Once we passed this type of training, it was time for field training. This was where the men were separated from the boys.

We stayed in field a week at a time in basic training. There, watch trainers showed us how to use our weapons, how to dig foxholes to live in. We all had water canteens. Our eating traces and food was in a can called sea racing. Some was good and some was bad, but we had to eat it. On Wednesdays, we got a hot meal brought to us by truck. They also brought mail; however, I never got mail because no one in my family knew where I was. We trained day and night how to fight in wartime. This went on for six weeks with no break or letup. The military broke us down to a child again and raised us again to soldiers. We were government property now. We learned to live with Mother Nature while in the woods. We came back to the barracks after a week in the woods. We were able to shower again and eat in the mess hall— that is, the lunch room. We could get off work at five thirty in the evening again. After one week in, were back in the field but longer this time—two weeks. We were learning how to live in the woods while fighting in combat. Later on, I was trained how to use other weapons such as the .45 pistol, rocket launcher, and heavy weapons. They sent us to the firing range to learn how to fire these weapons. After learning how to shoot them, we then had to go to the firing range to qualify with them. Went on a specially built range to learn how to fight with the bayonet. We fought dummies who sprung back when hit. We still couldn't get a pass to leave post.

Time moved on and toilingly we were introduced to the weapon that we would be using from now own. I qualified on the 75 mm recoilless rifle. It was mounted on a stand. Then a 105 mm rifle mounted on a Jeep. Later, I qualified on the 106 mm recoilless rifle. I was an expert operating these weapons. We were finally getting out of basic training. We played sports games, football, soccer, track, and other games. Now it was time to go and play games with other troops, just like in real war. The only difference was the bullets and bombs— we were blanks. This type of training went on for days. After this, I went to driving school and learned to drive a Jeep, 2 1/2 ton truck and a 3 1/3 ton truck. This was the first time I had been behind the steering wheel of an automobile of any type. This was exciting for me. I could now drive a car when I got out of the army. Now we were able to get a pass and go downtown, and this we did. On my first pass, I went with my buddies who were all White. We went to Junction City, Kansas, to go to the clubs and look the city over. After looking around town, we got hungry and looked for a place to eat. His is a story to be told forever. We went in this restaurant and were told that niggers could not eat in here. We discussed and decided to go in anyway. The manager came over and said, "I told you he could not eat in here."

We looked around and saw a lot of White soldiers were eating, so my buddies said, "We are going to eat," so he went back and sent a young White lady out to the table.

She said, "What do you guys want?"

My buddies placed their orders and said, "Give us double order with an extra plate."

She said, "No, I am going to feed this negro soldier too," so I placed my order. When she brought the order, the manager saw her serve me also. He called her in the back, and we saw him screaming at her, and she was screaming back at him. Now we didn't know if this was his daughter or an employee. She later pulled her apron off and left. So I became the first Black to eat in that place. I failed to get her name or the business name. I often wonder if she still remembers.

This is where soldiers worked hard to earn a pass to go to at night and weekends. You had to be back on base by ten o'clock and sometimes wake up at two o'clock for a special training. Basic training was not easy at all. You paid the price for enlisting in the army, but in the end, you realize why it was this way. You had to be ready to fight a war for this country, the United States.

We went through training that we never heard of. Looked like they were trying to kill us off. We became tough and tougher as the training went on. We got very little rest for six weeks. We learned every way we could kill the enemy in combat. That is what military is all about—learning how to fight during a war. We were trained to be killing machines. We trained how to kill the enemy seven days a week in basic training. We were trained by a number one West Point ranger. He was sharp.

My weapon, a 106 mm recoilless rifle. I learned everything about this weapon. The army said I was married to it, which meant I had to take care of it, and I did just that.

This is the weapon that I was an expert on. It was a tank killer. Each weapon had a name. My gun was named Hell Helper. There were three more in my platoon: the Nightmare, Ha Ta Trot, and Widow Maker. I was an expert with this weapon. I knew everything that you could know about it—that is, how to assemble it from scratch. My job was to destroy armor, such as tanks and bunker buster. I trained on other types of weapons. I was a sharpshooter with a .45 caliber pistol. I trained on the carbine and M1 rifle plus the .30 caliber machine gun and .50 caliber machine gun. All this training was not easy, but I was able to do it. All these weapons were to be learned to nilate the enemy in war.

Military weapons I trained on

Now it is time for precycle training. This training will last for sixteen weeks. My leaders were Lt. Willington Jr., a West Point ranger, Master Sgt. John Davidson, a war veteran, Sgt. First Class Brown, the only Black NCO in our platoon, and Sgt. Polskie. These platoon leaders are the ones who would train us to prepare to go overseas for Operation Gyroscope. We were going to Germany to replace the First Division (the Big Red One). We spent all but about three in the field these sixteen weeks. Would take you to the point of death so you would be able to sustain combat during wartime. We trained night and day without letting up, sometimes under live firing in some of these training ranges. We took ranger training, later some Special Forces training. There were times that I felt that I would be better off dead. At this time, we had gotten our marching orders and knew where we were going. We were told that we would be there for three years. In early September, we got fifteen days to go home after we had packed all our gears and supplies for shipping overseas. I went to Cincinnati, Ohio, on my way to Fort Dixie, New Jersey. My parents still lived in Alabama, and I didn't go to see them because I went over to Newport, Kentucky, and was told I could not drink from the same fountain as White people. I could not eat in the same place, and that I had to get in the back of the line at that store. Now I realized that the White people didn't respect me being in military uniform. I was still Black. So I didn't go to Alabama to see my parents because I was not going to apply with those Jim Crow statutes anymore; so I was not able to see them again for three years. At that time, they had moved to Cincinnati, and I was so glad to see them again.

This is the ship I went to Europe on, the USS *Randell*

In Germany

During this assignment, we were always on alert and ready to go. Now this was beautiful country. We enjoyed that part of our mission. The German people were all very friendly. There were some other military unites there also. We went to the clubs at night when we were off duty and had much fun. We were always looking out for spies from across the border. This was not a pleasure mission and we knew it. Once our replacement, we were off to another assignment. This time we went to Grafenwöhr, Germany. Our duty in Germany was to keep Germany stable after World War II. This wasn't easy. The German people still had lot of hate for us because of the war, so we were learning them and they were learning us. We had to learn some words in the German language. We had a manual that we carried with us so we could look in the book and see what was being said. This was another hard task for me traveling this journey in life, but I walked on looking for that brighter day in life. My mother told me that the road would be rough, but she taught me a name to always remember. That name is Jesus. She said he will be there when you need him, and she was right. I prayed to him during training.

The city of Bamberg, Germany. It is built around
water and beautiful streets.

I spent a lot of time in this city while living in Bamberg. There were a lot of clubs, which is what we GIs were looking for when we got a pass, and this was the first place that I went in a bar.

I pledged to defend and protect the United States and its
Allies Warner Barracks, Bamberg, Germany

The barracks I lived in in Bamberg, Germany, in 1955–1956

It is amazing how the military can strip you down to a child and train you to become a man different from any man in the street. You really become a fighting machine. Government issue, a GI—that's what it meant. From then on you are government property. No joke. My outfit was the last of the Tenth Division to be shipped out. There were people of all races in this country to see us off. They were waving and throwing kisses to us. The troop carrier was the USS Randall. As we boarded the ship, we knew we would not see the motherland for three years, if we were blessed to return. Away we went into the Atlantic Ocean. When we left the New Harbor, it looked as if the Statue of Liberty was waving at us, so we saluted. We were first going to England, then Germany. I was assigned special police duties on this ship. This was going to be a weeklong trip across the ocean. After being on the ocean for a week, we ran into a hurricane, and the ship seemed to be tilling over all day the first day. The next day was not as bad, but bad enough. I was assigning duty, which meant no one could go outside but the sailors, whose job it was to go outside. Some lady got outside as the ship real she was holding on to the when the sailors got to her and rescued her from going overboard. Now I was buckled to the wall by the door, but she didn't come out of my door. We got in other rainstorms but not bad ones. I did very good until we got in the English Channel, then trouble started. I got seasick. I can't really explain how sick I was, but I still had to work. When I laid down to sleep, it was as if my body was going up but my stomach was going down. This went on for a few days but I finally got over it. I got to see the White Cliffs of Dover, and they were beautiful. When we got in England—I believe it was called the South Panther—we were there for a few days, but I didn't like it because of the fog. After staying there a few days, we were loaded on a Tand heading for Germany. We arrived in Bamberg, Germany, where we would be stationed. Our post was Warner Barracks. This is where I would learn something about the other side of the world. My older brother had served here during World War II, also one of my father's brothers. We had to go to classes to learn what our duties were while serving in Germany. We were also given small books with some of the German language in it along with English, so we could learn to speak German. We had to learn the post which we were going to live on, so each day, they would take us on a tour of this very large military post. This was where all the stars were stationed when they had to serve overseas. Such stars as Bill Haley & His Comets, Gary Crosby, Bing Crosby's son, also Elvis Presley—just a few known stars. We went outside of the barracks to the fields and ranges to continue our training there. During this training, we would sometimes find unexploded rocket and booms that we would mar so the boom remover teams could come and destroy them. We were high-elevation soldiers, so we trained in the mountains. We were rapid-response troops, which meant we could be on the battle when needed in a very short time ready to fight for our country. While serving in Germany, I became a 2 1/2 ton truck driver. I drove from city to city transporting supplies to another military base in Germany; however, I was still in the heavy weapons platoon. We took terms pulling border guards with other military units stationed in Wildflecken. It was high in the mountains over the Fulda Gap area, just a small village. While stationed at Wildflecken, we encountered things we never dreamed of. We were so high up in the mountains the clouds would surround our barracks during the morning hours. We could look down and see airplane fly below where we were living. Military vehicles had to be repaired for high-elevation operation. We could see convoys of military trucks coming our way looking like ants crawling, and it took a day at least to get to the top of this mountain. When rain fell, it looked like a little ball of soft sleet. This was amazing. We stayed there six weeks, then rotated back to Bamberg, in Warner Barracks, our home base. If a war should break out with the Soviet Union, it would start here in the Fulda Gap, which separates Germany from Russell.

After being stationed in Germany, we still trained in different military bases. Wildflecken was a base high in the mountain. You could see airplanes flying below the mountain, and clouds would cover the barracks we stayed in. This was a military base where the army watched the Fulda Gap that divided Germany from Russell. Different military companies stationed in Germany were sent here every six weeks to observe Russell movement in the area. This mountain was so high you could see military convoys coming up to the base for days looking like little ants crawling up the hill. The population was five thousand citizens at the time when I was stationed there. We performed our duty as instructed.

Wildflecken, Germany

Moving to Grafenwöhr, Germany, this city was known as Mud City by the military because of the rainy weather which kept it muddy; and in winter, the snow got up to chest-high, and temperature was below zero most of the winter.

We were sent there to train in this weather so we would be ready to fight in this type of weather during wartime. During the time I was there, it was said to be the coolest winter in Germany history, December 1956–February 1957. It was sixty-five degrees below zero without a wind chill. I, along with other soldiers, froze. We slept in foxholes that had been dug by other soldiers dating back to World War II. We wore the military-issued clothing, but they just were not working for all of us, and I was one of them. There were tents all over the place in the woods, of course, because we were foot soldiers known as foot soldiers or boots today. There were warm-up tents, but once you went in one of these tent centers and went out again, it was worse on your body than before you went there. We played war games and trained daily, and that is when I got frostbite at its worst. So I would be sent back to Bamberg where I was stationed. My feet and hands had turned blue-black and swollen to extra-large size I thought they would take them off, but then they began to heal. I could not write home, so my parents got worried because they didn't know what had happened to me. My mother had the Red Cross to find me, so I got my buddies to write letters for me so I could write my mother. The whole time I was there, I only got mail from my mother, my friends Annie Robinson and Edna Sanford. My brother John had enlisted in the Marines, and he wrote me sometimes, and I would write him back to encourage him to hold on.

Grafenwöhr military base

Now we were back to home base in Bamberg. We still trained every day; it never stopped. We were ready for any assignment given us. One day it happened, there was one other assignment with the Tenth Infantry Division and it was real, not a war drill or training. About one o'clock in the morning, we were told to fall out in full combat gear. We were then told to load all our trucks with combat-ready supplies. When given the orders to move out, our platoon leader told us this was real. We rode till daybreak and at this stop, we assembled and got our orders that we would be receiving live ammo for all weapons. The company command also talked to us, and we thought that World War III was starting. We again were given the orders to move out and this time, stop at the Hungary border. We called this the forgotten war. As we waited for other orders, we now knew that we were going to face the real thing. This was in 1956. Before we went to Grafenwöhr, Germany, we were ready to face any army in the world. The Russians were on the rebels' side; America was on the side of the Hungary people. We waited and waited while talks went on with the United States and Moscow. Even though we went across the border, it was not considered a war, and we never got any re for prevent World War III from us who served in the military at that time and place. There was finally an agreement between the United States and Moscow. On October 23, 1956 was when it began, and the Soviet Union went into Hungary and crushed them. That was when we were put on alert to go to Hungary. These were the darkest moments of the Cold War. Washington finally made the decision the US would not enter into the uprising, so we returned to our base in Bamberg, and other troops returned to the base. We were ready if given the order.

Picture of war-torn Hungary in 1956

This uprising took place between October and November 1956. In December 1956 was when we went to Ravensworth, Germany, and I froze in that weather. In March 1957, I was transferred to Kaiserslautern, Germany.

Downtown Kaiserslautern, Germany

After arriving in Kapan Barracks in Kaiserslautern, I was assigned to the Forty- fifth AAA Third Battalion Battery B. Radar Platoon. I was the generator operator; this was a four hundred-cycle generator. It supplies electricity to the radar unit. The radar was the brain of the 90 mm guns. The gun ran off a sixty- cycle generator. I had to make sure that the electricity stayed at a stable level. I kept the fuel at a level required to operate the generator, also made sure the electric lines were properly working. The crew depended on me for their life. One thing about radar is it is spelled the same way backward as forward. That was the first thing I was taught. We were on the airplane destroyer miles before they got to the troop area to drop bombs or fire on the troops. I pulled this large generator with a 2 1/2 ton truck. We went off post to military movies, enlisted men's clubs and centers, but you had to earn a pass to leave the base. While in Bamberg, some of my buddies and myself started a singing group. This group was managed by Bing Crosby's son Gary, who was stationed at Warner Barracks.

He names the traveling show that he put together with the group and other entertaining "The Happy Valentine Show." They travel to all the military bases that were in Germany; however, I didn't travel with them because my but transfer but was with them when they came to Kaiserslautern EM Club. That was the last time I saw the group. I also had a good relationship with a young lady in Bamberg. Her name was Ann. She was from Italy. I was told by members of the group that she had twin girls, but they may not have been my kids. Now because I was from Alabama, the military separated us so we could not get married, because I was Black. I still wonder if I have twin girls in Europe.

While in Kaiserslautern, I got to see the Rhine River, the river that runs uphill. We did our training in Keil, Germany. That was the Submarine Base for the Germans during World War I. March 1958, I was transferred to the Twenty-Seventh AAA on the same base. These were mobilized guns on halt tracks. They were 75 mm guns and also had quad .50 caliber machine guns mounted on them, and I was the gunner on these machine guns. I was transferred because I was getting ready to come back to stateside. The Nike missiles were beginning to be introduced to the troops on this base, and they were doing away with the 90 mm big guns. I didn't get to train on the Nike missiles. I was glad to be coming back to the United States of America. While stationed in Germany, there was no racial problem with the German people liking Black soldiers, but a lot of them didn't like White soldiers. The German protests were screaming out, "Go home, Yankees. We don't need you in our country."

Overall, the Germans were nice to American soldiers. A lot of the women always wanted to talk about going to the United States someday. There were nice clubs to go to in Germany. Lionel Hamilton had a great there. The movie star Olivier Dehaven was born in Kaiserslautern, so she would come to visit us on the base from time to time. Landstuhl Air Force base was just a few miles from Kaiserslautern. The military main hospital in Europe was there also. My friend PFC Harold Watts and myself would go to the enlisted men's service club and play the piano to entertain the troops. We played what we called the double note. What this really was is both of us played the same piano together, and the soldiers loved the type of music we had developed. This was where I began writing songs. I wrote a song called "Soldier Boy Dream." This song made a big hit in the United States, but I could not get credit for it because I was in the military and you are government property, so you could not get any credit for any invention or song writing. Kaiserslautern was nicknamed Sin City. This was because of night clubs and legal prostitution. This was a wild city, and soldiers would take leave from other cities and come to Kaiserslautern. This was a beautiful city. The buildings and narrow streets were very beautiful.

United States military air defense is the greatest air defense in the world. They are equipped to defend our homeland 24-7. Their men and woman are well- trained for action. I served in the air defense when we first introduced the Ajax missile to Europe in 1958. I still remember the importance of an air defense to keep our great country safe. We have the best air force in the world today. Our defense team is ready at a moment's call.

Below is a radar united where the crew worked at and lived in whil

This is the crew that I was in, the Forty-fifth AAA Third Battalion Battery B. I enjoyed being in this crew. There only two Black soldiers in the crew, Sam Crush and myself. There were more Black soldiers in the gun section and ammo section. My best buddy was on the big gun. I served well for my country and was glad of it. Now it was time to leave Germany and come back to the good old United States of America. This was a long journey across the ocean. The ship was the USS Upshur, known as the tin can because of the continued sound of water hitting it. It was not like the larger ships. However, we were glad to be on any ship coming home back to the States. No more getting up at five o'clock in the morning or early in the night. I didn't know what to expect back home, but I looked forward to returning home. I would be going to stateside but will miss my buddies forever. I grew up with them all these years. We slept in the same room, we ate together, went shopping together. We did all things together, so they will be missed. The last unit that I served with in Germany was the Twenty-Seventh AAA. I was placed in this unit to be transported back to the

United States. I was in this unit for about three months. I was still in Kapaun Barracks.

75 mm AAA gun

Leaving Germany Going Home

A 90 mm AAA gun

The ship that I came back to the USA on

We loaded on the ship the USS Upshur, known as the tin can. This would be a two-week journey from Europe to the harbor in New York City. There was lots of rain but no storm like when we were overseas. As I looked, all I could see was mountains of water. It was like we were going uphill all the way across the Atlantic Ocean. We saw lots of whales following the ship, plus seagull birds followed us all the way home in the USA. These birds were amazing. They flew all the way across the ocean. When we finally saw the Statue of Liberty, it looked as if it was waving at us from the harbor. The torch was flying high, and we began to wave back at it and scream. As the tug boats tore the ship into port, there were people standing and waving, screaming and saying, "Welcome home!" Some of us cried and kissed the ground because we had spent three years or more away from home. We were transported to Fort Hamilton there in New York. I was shipped out to Fort Sheridan, Illinois, to the transportation unit. The base closed down in 1993. I was there in 1958. I knew that I would have to get used to civilian life. Because I grew up in the military, I had no street knowledge, just farm and country lifestyle. I didn't know one model of cars from another because I didn't see any of other type of automobile in Europe. I didn't see them while growing up in Alabama. I depended on family members to show me the way of life in the street. Some showed me the wrong way, but that didn't last long because I didn't like it. Just think, I didn't see a new car until I was in my midtwenties and didn't know the different make of cars. There were many things that I had not seen and had to learn about. I had never seen kitchen appliances and had to learn how to use stoves and electric equipment. I had to learn how to catch a street car and bus and how to shop at a supermarket. I was living on the same street with White people, not in a barracks in the military. It was a new world to me. I could talk to a White girl or woman without thinking about being hung. There were no KKK members burning crosses. And my parents had moved from Alabama to Ohio, but when I went to visit family and friends in Tuscaloosa, I still had to get in the back of the Greyhound bus from Kentucky to Alabama.

Fort Sheridan, Illinois

I was released from the regular army on March 12, 1958 to the Army Ready Reserve from March 1958 until July 1962. That is when I joined the Ohio National Guard in 1958.

I served during the Vietnam conflict in the National Guard and Army Reserve. I am a member of the American Legion, and my name is on the American Legion special soldier honor list.

These are some ribbons, awards, and division patches that I earned and served in while in the army, Army Reserve, and Ohio National Guard.

Above is some army unit that I served in and some ribbons and badges that I earned while serving in the military.

I arrived in Cincinnati, and everything was new to me—streets, buildings, and homes. I had to learn my way around town. It was hard. In May, I joined church services on Saturday. This is the Sabbath Sundown Saturday. This church was located at 1313 Center Avenue, next to a bar. I went to this bar all the time, and one day, a lady came in and invited me to this church, and that is how I became a member of this church. I found a job with this company, the Hamilton Diecast on Richmond Street there in Cincinnati, Ohio. I was a polisher buffer for the company. My pay was $42 a week. That was a pretty good salary for a Black person in those days. My parents had moved to Cincinnati when I got out of the military active duty. My brother-in-laws, along with one of my young brothers and myself, formed a gospel group named The Fairbanks Singer. That was the family's last name. We sung at different churches until I went to a group by the name of The Evening Shadows. In 1959, I got married, then joined another group named The Bible Tones. While singing with this group, I met the original Five Blind Boys, who wanted me to travel with them, but I refused to do so. In 1960, my friend and I founded Rev. Leon Hamner and the Holy City Travelers. That same year, I was ordained into the ministry. This group was a professional singing group. We recorded our first recording on KNOF Record located in Saint Paul, Minessota. KNOF was a radio station recording company. Floyd Author, out of

Hamilton, Ohio, was our producer. The hit song was "I'm Looking for a Man." It is still on the charts today, requested by many who passed the title down to their children.

My wife and I had our first child in 1961—a girl. I switched jobs because I needed to make more money. Went to a gas station, and they paid a little more $54 a week. Black people still could not get the same pay as White people. We still had to sit in the back of the bus in the South just across the Ohio River in Kentucky where I got my start as a teenager in the military. With my military- type life, I refuse to go back down South. I have gotten used to a new lifestyle in the military. It is a shame that the people that I went to protect the United States from treated me better than the White people did in my country. The German people showed Black soldiers much love but didn't like White soldiers that much. Now I am back to the Jim Crow era again. This is the same way it was when I went overseas. We still had trouble with the Whites in village and cities around Cincinnati. We would not go through the places after dark. The police would stop you with guns in their hands. I said to myself, *I should have stayed in Germany or at least in the military*. We couldn't rent or buy a home in the outer city of Cincinnati, just in what was called the Black communities. I looked for more work, but the most I could get paid was $2.10 an hour. I finally bought me a car, a 1955 Studebaker. I still was looking for a job paying better wages. Black people were still having race-related problems in Cincinnati, and I had a hard time adjusting. I had lived in Germany for three years without any type of race problem.

The church that I joined had Black and White members, but these White members would inform us on when was not good for us to visit because of their dislike for Black people. One of the bishops that ordained me was White Bishop Hogges, another bishop. On the Apostle Board was Bishop Gay Marvin Gay Father. I was ordained at Friendship College, in Rock Hill, South Carolina. The building was all wood and looked bad. The gym was leaning and rain leaked in it. There were no sidewalks, and it rained that week that I was there. Mud was everywhere This was a Black college. Blacks were still working in the cotton fields and farming for White people. We went to Bluefield, West Virginia, and some of the men worked in the coal mines for less wages than the White men were getting. It was very segregated there, and I was uneasy. Other hold time I was there, when I went to the store, I still had to get in the back of the line to shop. We didn't have to do that in Cincinnati, Ohio. White people would say "yes, sir" to us Black men. I will not forget going to Tennessee to a church meeting near Pinion Forge, and my youngest brother had just gotten out of the Air Force. We stopped to gas up, and while we were in the station getting a drink of water, they charged us 25 cents a glass. My brother went to the toilet and walked in the one that said Whites only. Within minutes, police officers were all over the place and had him against the wall. After talking to him, one was veteran and to him that Black people could not use the same toilet as White people. If this veteran had not been on that police force, there's no telling what would have happened to us. There were only six of us together, three men and three women. We could hear them talking about a nigger that went into the White people's toilet. While traveling with my singing group, we would stop to gas up in the country area of Tennessee, and they would not sell us gas. They would claim they was out of gas. White people was fueling up at the pumps and this was in the 1970s. Jim Crow was very much alive in parts of the South in the early '70s. I thought it would be better when I came back to the States, but I was wrong.

In Alabama, there were White people who felt like it was a disgrace for a Black man to have on a US Army uniform. They would ask him to take it off and not to wear it again. I was in the military from 1955 to 1963, so I didn't go down South anymore to live until 1994. Back to Cincinnati, Ohio, there was race no justly when it came to fare wages on a job, if you could find a good one. In 1965, I got a job with the City of Cincinnati, working at a water pollution control plant. With the city, I was paid $147 a week working in the sewage department cleaning sewage lines so they could run to the pollution plant. This was a very unclean job. I was married with three children to care for, so I worked with the City of Cincinnati until I had an on-the-job injury that kept me from working for over a year; but I was receiving worker's compensation for an income. When I went back to work with the city, the big boss, we called him, hounded me so much until I couldn't take any more, so I resigned from working for the City of

Cincinnati. I had a chronic back problem, which still affects me today. Lots of pain; however, I got in the BVR program and was assigned to work at Goodwill stores headquarters. Working for Goodwill, I was asked one day if I would like to get in a program that helped Black people get better jobs, so I said yes. My first assignment was a job at the Kent Corporation in Belleview Kentucky. They gave me a white partner who was on probation with the Probation Court in Cincinnati so we had to report to the Police Station there in Bellevue, Kentucky. Our shift was from six in the evening until two in the morning. Now I was the first Black person to work there. I was a spot welder building medical cabinets. When we got off work at two o'clock, the police would sometimes be out there to see us safe to the police station, so my partner could report out of the state. The employees did not want me there, so they complained, but the company kept me working there. The employees thought we were undercover cops. After someone saw us go to the police station, someone was selling drugs and thought we were trying to bust them, and this helped me stay there safe. The police escorted us to the Ohio River Bridge each morning. One day, everybody got a dollar raise but me. I was already making three dollars an hour. The White men who was doing the same job that I was doing, so I inquired about the raise. So I got a call about ten in the morning saying, "You don't have to report to work anymore. We have caught with our work." And this was a lie. To fire me, they didn't realize that they were firing my partner too because we were a team, and he could not leave the State of Ohio on probation.

After this job, I went to work for the Ohio Scroll Company as a wood carver. This was a good job, but I only got $4 an hour while the White guys got $6 an hour. This company moved from Newport, Kentucky, to Cincinnati. They repaired antique furniture. Again, these White guys didn't want me working there. They tried to get the company to make me a house cleaning person. There was a White person doing the house cleaning for them when I went there. I was there for about a year when a union spokesperson came by. But no one talked to him but me, so the company terminated me. I was the first Black person to work for this company, but before they let me go, they hired another Black man. After that job, I decided to get into security work. I worked for different companies. Finally, I worked in a Black-owned private police company. While working there, I worked in security for Lunken Airport and Cincinnati Convention Center. I got a chance to be a bodyguard for John Boy from *The Waltons*. The greatest thrill was when we became the Cincinnati Zoo police. There is where I met Neil Armstrong and be a bodyguard for him, the first man to walk on the moon. Then I was assigned to the State of Ohio OBES Building on Center Parkway. While working at the state building, I got work with some secret service agency because President Nixon was going to use center parkway to go to downtown Cincinnati. We were in contract with the state for a year.

Then the State of Ohio offered me a job with them. They were hiring retired city police and needed me to train them into the work program there, so I accepted the job and left the Crime Fighter Patrol, which was the private police company that I worked for. All this time, I was singing and recording with the Goldenaires of Cincinnati. We were a gospel singing group. We recorded on Champ Record, Su-Ann HSE Designers, HSE of America, and P.A.E.S. Records in Nashville, Tennessee. Before that, my group was Rev. Leon Hamner and the Holy City Travelers. We recorded on these recording labels: KNOF Record, Champ Record, HSE Record, Su-Ann Record in Nashville, Tennessee, and Designers Record in Memphis, Tennessee. I also had a church group named The Commandment Singers on Finch Recording in Cincinnati, Ohio. With the Holy City Travelers, we recorded three records. With the Goldenaires of Cincinnati, Ohio, I recorded seven records, and one record with The Commandment Singers. I recorded one records Altogether, I wrote just over one hundred songs and recorded ninety of them.

Back to the State of Ohio. I trained these retired police officers, but they didn't like it because they had never worked with any Black police. Cincinnati didn't hire Black police officers. The City of Cincinnati was now forced to hire Black people, so they were retiring the older White officers. Today, in the City of Cincinnati, they still have a police union, one for Black police officers and one for White police officers. There was one officer who didn't mind me training him. He was a sergeant in the Ohio National Guard. Later on, another retired police was hired, and we became best friends until he died. His name was Charlie Hunt. A few years later, the State of Ohio hired a female security police. Our headquarters was in Columbus, Ohio. In Cincinnati, they hired Penny Lewis, so McAllister asked me to train her for him. Mac was the boss for security. He said he had never worked with a female officer before s Black woman. The other White officers said they had never worked with a Black woman and was not going to now. I reported this to the Columbus office, so the chief of state security responded by saying, "You will work with her or resign." That ended that complaint. Chief Ernest was now retiring, so they replaced him with his son Ernest Ball Jr. The Secret Service Office had requested, but they would not let me wear a uniform or a badge. Chief Mill was very angry. He ordered me uniforms and a badge right away. The state started hiring Black security police officers, thanks to Chief Thomas Mill.

I was now getting the same pay as White security officers at my pay grade. I was assigned to the Cincinnati and Roselawn Bureau of Employment Services (OBES) office. Worked between them fourteen years. One day, there was problem with one of the White officers involved, so I wrote him up in my weekly report; but the manager of the OBES didn't want me to do so, but I did. It was requested that I be removed from the site, and Chief Mill asked me if I wanted to transfer. I agreed and was transferred to Batavia, Ohio, which was forty-two miles from where I lived, and there were no Black people living in this area. This was in 1986. Again, I was the first Black man to work in this office. One Black woman had been assigned there for a small period of time. There was no way I was going to move there because this was known as the KKK headquarters area. They still are there today in 2013. The office that I worked at was next to the state police office, so I worked hand in hand with them. I had no problem while working there for eight years. In 1994, I retired after twenty-two years with the State of Ohio. I accepted a job with Public Storage Inc. in Fort Wayne, Indianapolis, Indiana. I stayed there until January 1995, when my wife had a major heart attack, so we moved back to Alabama until her heart could heal. The muscles had to grow back, which took four years. After we moved back to Alabama, I got a job with Am Pro Protection Agency out of Columbus

S.C. who had a contract with the Michelin B.F. Good rich there in Tuscaloosa. In order to work for them, we had to go to medical school and become a certified EMT. I went to Alabama Fire College, which was a part of Shelton Community College in Tuscaloosa. I worked there for over a year as a security agent and EMT. We ran the emergency clinic there in this plant. There were 2,800 employees working there. After leaving this job, I became a private nurse for John Bishop, the founder of Dreamland Barbecue, a well-known eating place in Alabama. Mr. Bishop's daughter was now the manager of Dreamland. John Jr. also helped run the café along with her daughter. People from all walks of live came to Dreamland to eat. The sauce was the best. Today, the business goes on, but the Bishop family sold Dreamland.

Mr. Bishop became ill and was placed in Grandview Nursing Home in Northport, Alabama. I was his private nurse until his death. Also his wife, who was put in the same nursing home by their daughter, I was her private nurse. I also worked for Hugo Construction landscaping for new homes that were being built. The Hugos are still friends of ours. I work for harden Bakery for a while. I walked a mile and a half there and back in the rain, also in ninety-degree weather. We had to make a living so my wife could heal she would give relief at the nursing home with the Bishop family mother. I had to leave the bakery job because this job was still trying to fight against Black workers, and I couldn't take that anymore in life, so I got a job through Kelly Girls Spot Label Company. I went to work for the Coca Cola Company. During my deliveries in Green County, Alabama, I didn't realize that people were living the life of Jim Crow today. We delivered to a store where the White did not want me to be there. He said the driver had to take the drinks in the store because Black people could only come in this store on Wednesday. In the Salyersville, Alabama, area, we delivered drinks to a school where Blacks attended. The school was once a White school, but Blacks went there from the first through the twelfth grade all in this one school, while the White children had different schools for each grade level. There was no cable TV in the dirt road, just like how it was fifty years ago. I went to Akron Alabama black community, and saw Black people still on their knees picking cotton. They were waving at us as we passed by I could have cried. All of this was taking place in the '90s right there in Alabama; however, the City of Tuscaloosa was better, but still had their shortcomings.

During this period of time, I was still singing and was pastor of a church, Mt. Taber Baptist Church, there in Tuscaloosa. We would ride up to Peterson to see the old homestead. Someone has nature gas well on the property of the Hamner Hill. Don't know how long they have been doing this, but the property is still the Hamner Hill. My wife and I went a few miles in Peterson to see the script mine area, and it is still there. For a while, things got bad for my wife and I. She lost her memory for eighteen months, and I lost my job, so we would go shopping just looking around in the store so our friends wouldn't know how badly we were doing. We had no money. Sometimes we picked up pennies, nickels, dimes, and quarters off the ground in the parking lot so we could buy some jiffy meal and beans so we could eat. Now my wife would often say what she wanted for dinner, and, no joke, someone would bring it to us not knowing that we had no food to eat. This went on for a while, and thank God our social security disability came through and we were on our feet again. The Bible read that they that wait on the Lord shall renew their strength, and we did just that.

I hope whoever reads this portion of this book will gain more faith in God Almighty, because he is real. He proved it to my wife and me. If you keep the faith, God will bless you over and over again.

Before our disability came through, a friend named Scott—we called him Preacher Scott and he was a preacher—let us live in a house that he and his brother owned, which was their parents' home before they died. This house had holes in the floor. We covered them with carpet that we got out of the dumpster at night and dragged home. This dumpster was behind a carpet company, and we knew when they threw it out at night. We fixed this place up real nice, but it was very cold in the winter. We finally moved from there to McKenzie Court, in the projects. These were very nice apartments. We got behind on our gas bill, so they turned it off in the winter, so we borrowed coal oil heaters from our friend Scott for heating. We had electricity. There was a young man who had been watching us without us knowing it. His name was Billy. One day, Billy drove up to our home with a car and said, "I been working so you all can have some way to travel." This young man had been watching us walk to church at day and night plus going shopping and walking back with our grocery. We used his car for one year. It was a 1956 Oldsmobile. Billy showed up another day and said to me that God wanted him to pay me his tithes from his salary each payday, so he did that. We found out later that he was Preacher Scott's brother-in-law. There was a deacon of the church wife Sis Bonner who would let us use her car sometimes also. In 2010, I found out that Deacon Bonner died with a heart attack. There were those who helped us in times of need. The pastor's wife would let us use her car, and the pastor would come take it back. He would also keep the money that the church had taken up for me on Sunday sometimes.

When we were blessed with our back pay for our disability, we moved on up in life. I must tell you about when we first got to Tuscaloosa. I had a car, and while asleep one night, our talking parrot, who was given when he was a baby bird (my wife named him Paul), woke my wife up at two in the morning to let her know something was going on outside. But my wife didn't wake because I was working a twelve-hour shift six days a week. When I got up at six in the morning for work, my car was gone. The parrot tried to tell my wife, but she didn't look outside. We moved in a nice house near Stillman College and stayed there for one year, and the landlord sold his house, so we had to move so he could move in this house he rented us. God blessed us, and we were able to buy a house in Albert City. We also owned three automobiles—two cars and a station wagon. I was pastor of a church also. This is when I met Mr. Hugo and his family. Mr. Hugo offered us a home for free in the country, but my wife didn't like living in the country, so we didn't accept it. The pastor's wife of our home church mother died and left her home for us. Also, God was blessing us in many ways. My wife had no family members in Tuscaloosa, but there were some family members in Birmingham and Montgomery, Alabama. She had death in her family in Hamilton, Ohio, so she went there for a month. She called me and said that she would like to move back to Ohio, but I said no, so she said, "How about Indianapolis, Indiana?" I agreed to that suggestion. We made plans and decided to move to Indianapolis, Indiana.

Leaving Alabama was not what I really wanted, but I moved her closer to her family. She had only been to Indianapolis about three times before we moved there, but her daughter, my stepdaughter, lived in Indianapolis with her family. I had been in and out of Naptown since 1960. I had some family members living there, plus my singing group had been in the city of Indianapolis lots of times. My wife and I were trained there when we went to work for Public Storage. I sold one of the cars before I left Tuscaloosa and hit the road for Indiana. When we got to Indianapolis, the car we still had broke down. It just quit running, period, and we was walking again. I said to my wife, "We walked off and left our blessings, so we will make do with what we have."

Living in Indianapolis, Indiana

Indianapolis is a nice city to live in; however, we had our problems. There were ten shootings this past weekend, January 30–31, 2016. All young people shooting one another most on the inter east side. We need some type of gun control for selling guns on the streets. The city of Indianapolis has an all-around sports town. We have professional football, soccer team, men and women professional basketball teams, pro hockey teams, and baseball teams. Don't forget the Indiana Speedway 500. I live about three miles from the racetrack.

To here

This is the home I live in today, November 2020

Moving from there to here is where I live at now in Indianapolis. We moved here in August 1999. Things changed from where we lived in Tuscaloosa, Alabama. We lived in Aspen Village Apartment for one year, then moved in a senior citizen building. Our car quit on us, so our daughter-in-law we call Rock in Hamilton, Ohio, gave us a station wagon. It lasted for a little while, then it broke down, and I said again to my wife "We have left our blessings," but she did not want to return to Alabama. The house we were buying in Tuscaloosa was blown away in the great storm that hit that city. We live in the Crock Creek Tower Senior Citizen on Michigan Road in Indianapolis where I work part-time as an assistant residence employee. We watch and take care of the property at night and weekends.

Crock Creek Tower

We lived for five years on the seventh floor, and it was a very good place to live. The Metro Bus service was just across the street and a shopping area was within walking distance. We enjoyed living here, but after I became ill and could not ride the elevator or walk up the steps, we had to move to another senior apartment on the second floor. We moved in the Georgetown Station Senior Apartment. This was a nice place to live also. We were still having car troubles. Our son gave us a car, but the motor went bad o it like always another person gave us a car a church member named Larry Brow. We still have that car today because it still runs good, plus it is an antique. This apartment was also on the Metro Bus line so we rode the bus often. We joined a church while living at Georgetown Station. This is our home church as of now, One Vision in Christ Community Baptist Church, same church that Larry Brown belonged to. This church was a mix of Blacks and Whites. Larry Brown was White and is a great friend of ours today. The Goldenaires are retired and all, but three members have ended their journey on earth, and God has called them home. However, you can still hear our recordings. In March 2008, we received a Lifetime Achievement Award from C.U.L.A.N Inc. In 2008, we also recorded the CD Standing the Test of Time. In 2011, June 8, we were inducted into the Gospel Music Workshop of America Hall of Fame. For me, this was a great achievement coming from life during the Jim Crow era in the Deep South. We recorded over one hundred songs and travelled to many cities plus thirty-five states here in in the United States of America.

Once I moved to Indianapolis, it looked as if I finally got away from racism.

We still have a long way to go, but it is better. We made progress since living in Indianapolis, Indiana. We have our own home near Butler University. At this point, I am legally blind, but that's okay. God has been good to me. I made it to seventy-seven years, by his grace. I been a preacher of the gospel for fifty-three years, recording gospel songs for fifty-three years as of now. I am a cancer survivor, thank God. I am the father of seven children and five stepchildren, but still I've come a long way to get to where I am today. I keep hope alive for my people in America and know that a change will come in this great country so Black people will have real freedom. We were once considered not human, sold like merchant products on the market, and never had real freedom. Even today, there are some areas in the state of Indiana that I will not even stop in because the Ku Klux Klan are still very much alive in some of these are racial that groups right here in Indianapolis, and we know that to be true. I am blind legally, but when I entered the store to shop with my two stepsons, this store employee followed us all over the store profiling us because we were Black men and she was White. I do not blame all White people for such actions, but this must be pointed out this was a Saver-A-Lot Store. We Black people are still not trustworthy to some White people. We as a people will not go back to the Jim Crow lifestyle in this country. Our children and grandchildren Black and White will make sure we don't. You can see the change coming already. Look at how many names Black people have had in this country. How can we teach our children what race we really are when our race name changes like the wind, just nass confusing. We been called 1) nigger, 2) negro, 3) colored people,

4) Black people, 5) Afro-American, and 6) people of color. I wonder what is next. Now it is time to move on in life in a great country of the free and brave. This is the greatest country in the world, and yet Black citizens are not yet free as White people. There are some running for president of the United States who want White supremacy back. That is what they mean when they say we are going to take America back, speaking in code.

Moving on in Life

As life moved on, I had a lot of ups and downs. I still see racial problems in America It is still hard for Black people to get home loans in an upper- class community. Blacks still have to except lower-paying wages on jobs. Let me take a look at my life from there to here, after leaving Peterson,

Alabama, going from dirt roads to streets and sidewalks. I first learned to walk on a sidewalk in Cincinnati, Ohio. I saw a sidewalk in Fort Riley, Kansas, in the US Army. Fort Riley is where I first began to experience life. I was not aware of how a person could live. My clothes could be sent to a cleaner, something I never dreamed about as a child. I had heard my father the cleaners in town Tuscaloosa, Alabama. In Cincinnati, when I visited there at fourteen years old, there was a cleaner down the street from where I lived a few weeks with my sister and her family. In Alabama, I saw only one-floor houses or shacks for homes, but when I went to Cincinnati, I saw tall buildings. My sister lived on the third floor and I thought that was great. No snakes crawling in the house, no leak where you had to sit a bucket to catch the water. There was a bathtub, something I hadn't seen before. I had to learn how to turn water factures on at age fourteen. I learned how to flush a toilet. Also I might sound but that is the way it was. I went to the movie with my brothers, Riley and John. We stayed there most of the day. I got to see a real train station and bus station. As a young man, I didn't know anything about street life because I was raised in the woods and knew every trail and road in that area. I knew all about farm life and country living but had to learn how to turn on an electric light, had to learn about traffic lights and street lighting. I learned how to ride a city bus in Germany at age eighteen. I saw a washing machine for the first time in Cincinnati, also my first gas stove along with a heating system.

Downtown Cincinnati, 2020

Cincinnati Music Hall 2020

At age eighteen, I took my first shower at Fort Knox military base in Kentucky. This was a thrill. I went to a barber shop for a haircut for the first time in my life. Can't you see what type of life I had to live growing up through the years? I was able to drink water from the same fountain as a White person, shop in the PX without going to the back of the line. I could now sit in the same café with White people for the first time in my life. I was still a little shaky because I was afraid of White people and running from them. Now you see that I was raised in the United States Army. Moving on, entered Germany, and this is where things changed my life. My first dating was with a young lady from Italy. We dated for a year, and the army transferred me and I didn't see her again. I could look at a White woman and not be whipped or hung. I had money in my pocket for the first time in my life. I wrote and told Mother about how things were, and she wrote back and said that god had heard her prayers. I had come a long way to get to where I was. I cried lots of times and wiped tears away. I went from the army active duty to the Army Ready Reserve, then the Ohio National Guard. Today, I am a member of the America Legion. Now the rest of my life story. After returning from active duty overseas, I joined Progressive Baptist Church with my parents, who had moved from Alabama to Cincinnati. I later joined the Church of the Living God, which is still my mother church home. I was ordained and licensed in 1960, at the age of forty- four at the Assembly of the House of God at Rock Hill College, Rock Hill, South Carolina. I also recorded my first record in 1960 on KNOF Record, Saint Paul, Minnesota. This group was Rev. Leon Hamner and the Holy City Travelers. The song was "I'm Looking for a Man," which was a hit recording. It is a gospel classic today. I have traveled to thirty-five states here in the United States and five foreign countries since leaving Alabama. I have visited some of these states more than ten times while traveling and singing. While on the road, we found out that racism was still alive. In the '60s, while traveling, we experienced not being able to buy gas at a service station, had to pay for a drink of water, could not stop to shop in rural area stores, and still saw signs with racial tones along the highway.

Edward R. Leon Hamner Sr.

Country road in Tennessee

We saw fields where KKK cross had been burned. There were Black people

working in the field, just like they were when I was a child. They would wave at us as we rode by. Leaving Ohio, we would get angry but kept it to ourselves. I saw signs along the road in Alabama in the '80s, again in the '90s, that said TNT, for "Trot, nigger, trot." This was just north of Birmingham, Alabama. You could see this sign from the Greyhound bus as you pass by.

KKK cross along the roadside

Today, 2015, you can still see these KKK crosses in fields in northern states, including the state of Indiana. In 1959, I got married and we had five children—four girls and a son. I worked at a gas station for a year. I was also in the National Guard. I made $2.10 an hour while working at this gas station. My wife also worked. This was how we took care of our family. My wife made $1.50 an hour. Life was very hard then, but we made it somehow. I was singing and preaching in and out of town. I bought my first home in Mount Auburn in Cincinnati, on Channen Street. Went to work with the City of Cincinnati in 1965. I worked in the sewerage department on the road crew. I made $147 a week, the most money that I had ever made in my lifetime. During the time I worked for the city, White employees made more money than Blacks because White men had all the management and supervisor jobs, and we Black men were still laborers. I worked during the week and traveled and sung on weekends. We didn't make much money singing. At most, we earned about $200 a show and split it among six members. We always booked at least two shows a weekend, plus with record sales, we made about $600 a weekend. The record company took all our royalties from Black recording artist. In 1968, I got injured on the job while working with the City of Cincinnati. Two of my fellow workers had been killed while working with the city. One got killed in the sewer trap by gas; the other one was killed at home. Our job was to keep the raw sewerage flowing to the sewerage plant from all areas of the city. This was a very dangerous type of work and still is today. I got a serious injury from a fall and still suffer from it right now, with chronic back pain. I was out of work for a year and then from time. I couldn't do that work anymore so I went to rehab. At Goodwill for one year before I could look for work again. I go to Goodwill even today to shop because of the way they helped me when I was not able to work. I got hired working for General Security Agency and was assigned to the federated stores in Cincinnati in the Northgate area. While working there, the Brink's truck came and picked up the cash but left a bag with $100,000 in it. My supervisor called them when I turned the money in, but Brink's said it was not their money, but we knew that it was. So the federated store finally convinced them to come back and get it. They think the management, not me, was the one who found the money. They could not believe a Black man had found this unmarked money and turned it in. I got a better job working for Pinkerton Security, getting paid $42.75 an hour. We are talking about wages in the '70s for Black men. In 1969, I had a divorce but remarried in 1971, and we had two children—a boy and a girl. I worked for America Security, where I was in training under the GI Bill, which I got paid from both the company and government. I was still traveling and singing on the weekends. The group was recording on Designers Record Label in Memphis, Tennessee. Style Wooten was our producer. Designers has released some of our recordings on the Soul of Designer Record. It was released in September 2014. It can be bought at Amazon. My group was Rev. Leon Hamner and the Holy City Travelers.

That's my picture, on the lower right-hand corner of this label, with the coat over my shoulder. Style Wooten is next to me. The *Wall Street Journal* had a small write-up about me and other recordings on Designer label in the December 2014 issue. The Holy City Travelers recorded on this label until 1971 1971 Dec. Jesse Willingham founded the Goldenaires of Cincinnati, Ohio. I joined the group in 1972. They had not started to take programs as of yet. I was the only professional recording artist in this group. I began to write songs for the group in 1972. The group recorded their first record on Champ Records in Nashville, Tennessee, on Church Street. We decided to name the LP "I've Come a Long Way." The song "I've Come a Long Way" was a hit song. It played seven days a week for one year on the radio station

WLAC in Nashville, Tennessee. It was playing on a lot of other gospel and Christian radio stations,

Black and White stations. Our backup musician was from the Marter Roberts Bank. The record has a bit of country and Western music on each song. I was returning home from a show in Tennessee and stopped at a truck stop and was looking at some items. A White lady walked up to me and said, "You look like someone I know." I asked her where she was from. She said, "I am from Alaska."

I then joked, "You might have seen my recording."

She, to my surprise, said, "That's it. I bought a record name 'I've Come a Long Way.'"

I smiled and said, "Yes, that's my recording." She was so thrilled she went to some other people telling them who I was, but I had to leave and get back home, so I left while she was still talking about our recording.

The original legendary Goldenaires

The Goldenaires went on recording in Nashville, Tennessee, through 1984. We recorded for HSE, Su-Ann, and HSE of America. We traveled to many towns and cities singing and spreading the gospel. In the early '90s, I also sang with Original Blind Boy of Mississippi. Back to my life moving on. During the civil rights movement, I worked for Swanson Furniture. Paul Trottman was the owner. I was the first Black to work for the company, and he paid me good. Sometimes I made $600 a week. I worked for the Kent Corporation in Bellevue, Kentucky, as a spot welder. The White guys made $3 an hour, more than I did doing the same job. One day, I found out that all the employees had gotten a one-dollar raise but me. Now one employee and myself were the two welders in the company, so I inquired about the raise and they fired me. I was the first Black person to work for the company. The Ohio Scroll Company moved from Kentucky to Cincinnati, and I got hired by the company. I was a carver. We repaired antique furniture. Again, the White employees were making $3 an hour more than me. I inquired about this, and again they fired me. It was still hard for Black people to make the same wages as White people. I was caught up alone with Father in the middle of the 1960 riots in Cincinnati, Ohio. My brother Paul lived one block from where it all started. It was a mess there in Avondale. They burned down every business in the area that was Black-owned, but it was a 99% Black community. Today, June 1, 2015, they never built the business area back. That part of Avondale is still a ghost town. In 1974, I got a job with the Crime Fighters Patrol, a Black-owned privative police and private investigation agency. This agency had lots of contracts. I worked as security for Lunken Airport, Cincinnati Convention Center. We became the Cincinnati Zoo police.

Neil Armstrong on the Moon

I was a bodyguard to Neil Armstrong and was so thrilled that I was a bodyguard of the first man who walked on the Moon. I remember when I was a child, we sat and talked about the man on the Moon. When I look back over my life during the time I lived in Alabama, I never thought that I would be guarding the man on the Moon. When you are walking along this journey in life, you never know what tomorrow will bring. Will it be sunshine or will it be rain? Well, I have had both during this journey in life.

Moving On

Center the Walton had a display at the center and was a member of the convention center security team, and my job was to be a body guard of John Boy. I enjoyed this. You see, my name is Hamner also, and all Hamners are related, Black or White. John Boy was very, very nice and enjoyed looking at all the other displays at the center.

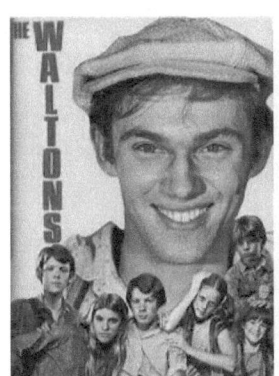

The Cincinnati Zoo is a landmark in this city. People come from around the world to visit this zoo. I loved working at this zoo and assisting people while they visited the zoo.

We served as police and first-aid officer. The zoo was a great place for working with the public. I had work across the street from the zoo as property manager for Dural Avenue Apartment Twin Towers. The State of Ohio hired me while I was assigned there by Crime Fighters Patrol. They needed security at the OBES office in Cincinnati on Center Parkway. The City of Cincinnati was retiring the police officers who had been there for years, so they created jobs for them with the State of Ohio. This was happening in many cities in Ohio. I was working with a contract at the state OBES building. The state hired me, and when they hired these police officers, I was the person who had to train them on this job site. During this, the Secret Service was in the area because President Nixon was coming to Cincinnati, and he was taken by the state building where I was working. I had a young man just out of the marines working under me, and we called the Secret Service agent there with the man from Unclew. When the president had left Cincinnati, the man from Unce whose first name was Richard, when he was leaving, he gave me a copy of a letter that had sent to Columbus Ohio the headquarter form my job. The letter said that I should be given the job position that was open as chief of security, but the state didn't do that. They gave the position to the retiring chief's son. When these retired police from the City of Cincinnati started to be hired, I started training them, and they made at lease $5 an hour more than I did. This happens on job sites today. Black people train White employees on jobs and they are removed, and the White person gets the job that this Black who trained them had. I trained six police officers on this job site, but the State of Ohio would not issue me a uniform or badge. Went on for years. After I trained these offices, they tried to put me in the maintenance department. They put me in the parking lots. The chief officer job was open again, and the state ordered them to issue me a uniform and badge.

They hired a female Black woman. These ex-police protested, but it didn't do any good; she got the job. These ex-police said that they had never worked with a woman police and was not going to start now. I had to train her on this job site, and they worked with her. She got another job assignment. The female was working the Roselawn OBES office, and she went to another job, not with the state of Ohio. I became the local union president of the Ohio Workers' Union, where I argued with the State of Ohio for part-time employee worker rights. We won the rights for sick leave, vacation leave, personal leave, and more. I was transferred to the Roselawn office to replace a female officer. While working there, the State of Ohio closed down a lot of small OBES, so I had to transfer files to other offices in Hamilton County, Butler County, and Clermont County. Later in the year, the State of Ohio closed the Roselawn office and moved those employees to Cincinnati OBES office. That meant that I was back to the Cincinnati office. I was still having problems with some of these police officers. I was now the executive secretary for the board of directors for the Ohio Public Workers' Union. One day, I wrote up an employee for being drunk on the job, so they had a meeting and asked me to withdraw this document, and I refused. So they had one of these offices write up a document to call my document wrong, and he did, but when the meeting was held about this, I won the case because the employee told them that I was correct that he was drinking alcohol on the job, so they put him in a rehab program to this his job, which is what I wanted.

After this was all over, they asked me to be transferred to Batavia, Ohio. They thought I would say no because this was a known area for KKK home base in Southern Ohio. I took the assignment and worked with the state police, at Post 32. I was the second Black person to work at that OBES state building. After working there for one year, the State of Ohio said that they didn't need my job position anymore, but when they laid me off, they had to lay off all employees with the job title that I had. Before this, they laid me of on disability leave for three years but had to bring me with credit for all three years on the last layoff. I filed a complaint through the union, and the union went through all courts all the way to the State of Ohio Supreme Court. I won in all courts. So this took two years, and they had to rehire me and others with two years back pay with interest. I have already stated that I worked at this job site for eight years. I traveled eighty miles a day to go back and forth from work but got no travel pay. I was punished for writing a manager at the Cincinnati office. I applied for more than fifty jobs for the State of Ohio, but they would not hire me because they were told not to hire me. I applied for a veteran representative job, and the manager turned in the request to hire me, but they told her to take my name off her list. She refused, so they had several meetings with her. She still refused to remove my name, so they removed her from that site in Middletown, Ohio, and sent her to the Cincinnati office. She and I were the only ones who knew why she was removed from the manager job in Middletown.

In 1994, I retired after thirty-four years of public work, but the state did not give any retirement pay because they said I owed the retirement board money, but they would not let me pay the amount that they said that I owed. Today, I got no pay for my public service work. I worked 3 1/2 years for the City of Cincinnati, 1 year for Hamilton County Park District, 22 years for the State of Ohio, and 8 years in the military. No retirement pay. Back to when the state placed me on a three-year disability leave without pay, I worked as operation manager for the radio station WAIF 88.3 FM in Cincinnati,

Ohio. I then went to work for the Hamilton County Park District. While working for the Hamilton County Park District, I made honor employee of the month and was on the front page of the paper. These ex-police that I had worked with just couldn't stop. They gathered up copies of the park newspaper and sent them to Columbus, Ohio. Don't know why they did this, but whatever; it didn't work. After retiring from the state, I went to work for Public Storage Inc. as property manager in Fort Wayne, Indiana. I had three assistant managers under me; my wife was one of them. I had six hundred storage bins and had them leased at 99 percent. When Public Storage switched their system over to a computerized system, they chose my site to do it. This was a new system. We had to learn how to work with it, and we did in a timely period. My wife had a major heart attack, and we moved back to Alabama until she recovered. This was from January 1995 to August 1999. Well, it is time to look over what we been writing about. We will call it Then and Now. I want you to compare life during the Jim Crow era with life today, with Black citizens' lives in America today. Then was not the way God wants us to live. He wants us to walk together as his children, not hating one another, so let's look at the Then and Now. Just a few examples.

1. Transportation

Then

Growing up in the Southern United States, Black citizens had to ride in the back of the bus. Where I lived, there was no city bus. Only the Greyhound bus came through Peterson, Alabama. When we caught that bus, we rode in the back. I was told about Black people riding in the back of the bus. The driver of the Greyhound bus lived in Peterson. They drove from Tuscaloosa to Birmingham, Alabama.

Now

Now we move from the back seat to the very front seat, next to the driver of the bus. I went back to Tuscaloosa in 1985–1999, and the bus drivers were Black. I didn't see a White city bus driver. Riding the Greyhound bus, lot of drivers were Black bus drivers. The only other bus that I rode in was a school bus, and all the children were Black children.

1. Shopping

Then   Now

Then

We had to go to the back door of the store to shop. Black people could not use a front door to any White business. Of course, they owned all businesses downtown. Some of these stores, you could go shopping there once a week, on the assigned day for Black people to shop. There were some nice grocery stores in downtown Tuscaloosa.

Now

Nowadays, Black citizens can shop at any grocery store in the United States. We can enter at all entrances to the store. Not only can we shop, but Black people also manage some of the greatest grocery stores in the country. There are some grocery and other stores owned by Black people; clothing businesses, gas stations, hardware stores. My oldest brother owns a hardware store in LA, California. All types of businesses are owned by Black people.

1. Working

Then

This was the work that followed Black people all their life during the Jim Crow era. We did all the farming for White people, and they kept the money that we made for them. I saw how hard my mother and father worked. I worked hard myself in these fields. Black people did other types of work. They worked in coal mines, railroads, sawmills, and at White people's homes. Some work in sharecropping. Our family did once.

Now

Black citizens work in offices, are hospital doctors, nurses, in maintenance, housekeeping, and the list goes on. We have the same jobs as White people, even becoming president and vice president of the United States of America. We are not the semislaves that we were during the Jim Crow era.

1. <u>Education</u>

Then

Going to school in those days was miserable; no heat, no air-conditioning, no very good desks, if any at all. There were times we sat outside under the shade of the tree for class because it was too hot in the church where we went to school in. There were sheets to divide the classrooms, and one teacher who taught the first though the fourth grade. When we went to junior high school, it was in a building, but still had potbelly heaters for heating, no electricity, no running water, and an outhouse for toilets. In high school, we had electricity but no running water, and still heated the room with potbelly heaters. We still had an outhouse for toilets. In grade school, we had to bring our lunch from home. And there was no lunch room to eat in. We sat at the desk and ate.

Now

Schools nowadays have convenience at its best; central heat and air, very good desks and seats, computers and tablets, all electronic equipment, bathrooms, water, and a lunch room. There is a library, study hall, and textbooks for every class. Some schools have uniform to wear, which I think is great. There is a first-aid clinic in some schools that I know of. No child has to go hungry. There are food programs that make sure that children can get a hot meal.

2. Housing

Then

Take a good look at this home. I saw this type of home with my own eyes because we lived in one like this. Now no one paid rent because Black people built their home with what they could get from sawmills. Some found old lumber left by lumberjacks in the woods. There was no mortgage payment. We didn't have an address or roadside mailbox. Most or all families were large. These homes didn't have electricity or water or any type of utility. We all had a fireplace, a potbelly heater, and wood and coal burning kitchen stove. Most windows were shutters, no window pane. You opened these shutters every day during summer so the wind could circulate through the home. Some people still own these houses. I know three families who still live in Peterson who live in them, but they have electricity and running water, also an inside bathroom.

Now

This home has everything a family needs in it—two or more bathrooms, electricity, running water, and all other utilities that are needed. There is an attached garage and family room. Some have a home office in them (I do), central heat and air, also laundry room. When you look at these two homes owned by Black citizens, you realize that we have come a long way, but we still have

3. Healthcare

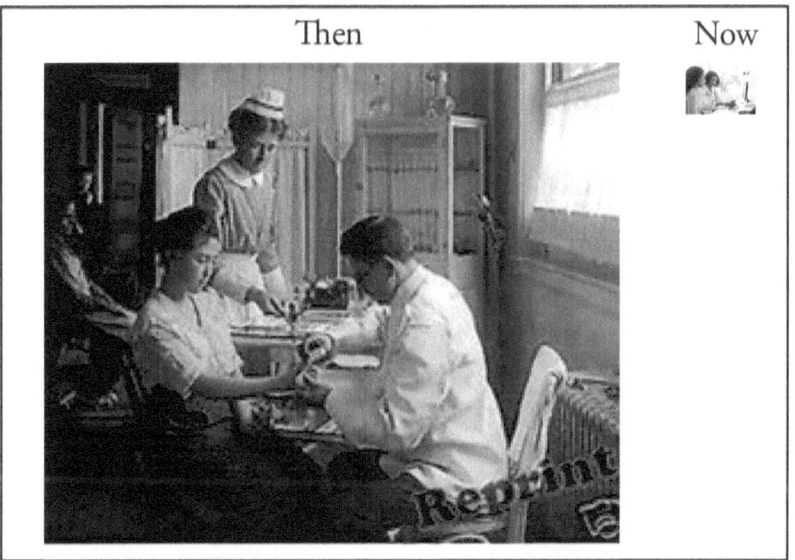

Then   Now

Then

There was only one Black doctor in Tuscaloosa County, Dr. McKenzie. His office was about fifteen miles from where we lived, and we had not transportation to go see him, so our mother took care of us when we got sick. She also took care of the White and Black families when they were sick. She was the midwife. Also the people in Peterson called her Doctor Yank. Today, a street in Tuscaloosa is named after him. Also a housing complex is named after him.

My wife and I lived in this complex. There was one hospital that admitted Black people. It was North and General Hospital. It was located between Tuscaloosa and Cottondale. The name was changed, and they turned it into a veteran hospital.

Now

Now we have some of the best hospitals in the world where Black citizens can get the medical care needed. There are seven hospitals in Indianapolis, Indiana, that I know of. We have one of the best VA hospitals that the United States has for veterans. There is an EMT life squad who does a great job getting people to the hospital. That is what I was when I retired—an EMT. There are great children's hospital for our children, and a lot of clinics, some owned by Black people. We don't have to go to the back room in the hospital anymore and wait until White people have been served.

Civil Rights

T he right of citizen to political and social freedom and equality. The term civil rights refers to the basic rights afforded, by laws of the government, for every person, regardless of race, nationality, color, gender, age, religion or disability. This refers to such rights as equal citizenship, equal protection under the law and due process. Examples: civil liberties, freedom of speech, freedom of the press, freedom of religion, freedom to vote, etc. Civil rights in the United States 1964 Act is a landmark civil rights and labor law in the United States that outlaws discrimination based on race, color, religion, sex, or national origin. It prohibits unequal application of voter registration requirement.

Source: Library of Congress

Black Americans have marched and protested for many years. White Americans have also marched with Black people and died trying to get equal rights for Black citizens. White racial hate groups are back in the streets without long guns strapped to their shoulder, but Black and White citizens have no fear of them; they keep protesting in large crowds. Today's generation is not like it was years ago. These young people have come up in school together, worked together, lived together, and don't see Black or White people. They just see their friends and sisters and brothers. They are going to change race relationship in this great country.

We finally made it to "here." It was a long journey, the road was rough and rocky, the hills in life were hard to climb, but through it all, I made it. Jesus never let me fall.

We have a ways to go still. The freedom we Black citizens have is good, but we're not there yet, so we'll keep on climbing until we reach the top of this mountain in life. I can see it. Our children will enjoy it.

years in the EU Department. I served as district chaplain for the Universal Brotherhood, Masonic and Eastern Star Lodge St. Joeshop#2, where I served at Cincinnati, Ohio. My life is serving God to the end of my journey. God has been good to me and my wife, Ornette Hamner. We own two homes in Indianapolis, I have my business, I am a BMI publisher, Heaven Helpers Music CEO, and affiliate publisher for merchant partner, Grandpa Hamner Place at ehamner.com or grandpahamnerplace.com. I published over two thousand businesses on the internet. I have seven children, and all of them went to college. My wife, Ornette, was a nurse assistant and property manager for public. We thank God for his goodness to our family and our achievements in life.

Life Today

Today I live a wonderful life with my wife, Ornette, have had four cancer surgeries, and two stomach and two colon surgeries. I have had any treatment or medication I been five years since the last surgery. I also had kidney failure and three light strokes, but by the grace of God, I am still standing. I remember the song my mother sang daily, "There's a Bright Side Somewhere." Don't you stop until you find it. There is a bright side somewhere, thank I found it that is a bright side. I sing it in my heart for my children, grandchildren, and great-grandchildren. In my heart, I want them to find it like I did. I am still walking on my journey home to live with God. My life changed in the early '60s. I walked into the religious world of life. I begin in the ministry in 1960. I preached my first sermon at 134 Street, Baptist Church during the House of God convention. I was ordained in August 1960 at Rock Hill College during the House of God convention. After that, I traveled from town to town and city to city preaching and singing. I started singing with a local group named the Evening Shadier, the Bibletones Singers. I already had a church group named the Commandment Singer, and we recorded in Flinch Records. In 1960, we had another gospel group, Rev. Leon Hamner and the Holy City Travelers. We recorded our first professional record on KNOF Records out of Saint Paul, Minnesota (I'm Looking for a Man). It became a hit record and the group label number two in the gospel recording field. We traveled on the road singing to large and small crowds. The group stopped recording in 1971. At that time, we had three hit records on the market. In 1972, a friend of mine came to me and said, "I need you. I am organizing a gospel group and need a lead singer." So I accepted the offer. He named the group Goldenaires, and we recorded until 2008, and we had five hit songs. We recorded six LPs, we traveled to thirty-five states in the United States. I also sang with the original Five Blind Boys of Mississippi. I worked five days a week, and we sang on weekends.

I pastored three churches and was an assistant pastor for two churches. I was pastor for First Baptist Church in Lincoln Heights, Ohio, Second Holiness Church in Cincinnati, Ohio, and Mt. Tabor Baptist Church in Tuscaloosa, Alabama, and assistant pastor at Truth Missionary Baptist Church in Cincinnati, Ohio, and The House of God at the Vine Street mission. I was a member of the National Chaplain Association, where I was ordained a minister at Grace Baptist Church and received a church charter. I was a volunteer chaplain at the University of Cincinnati IU Hospital.

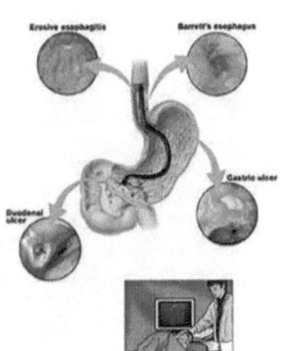
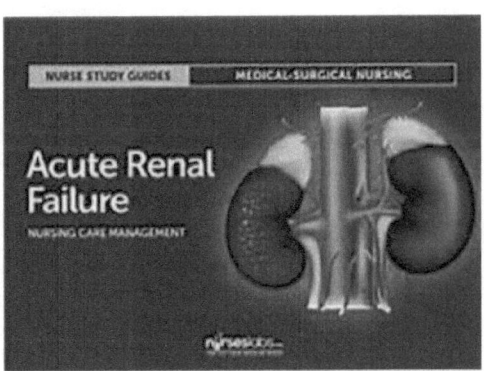

Summary

I have written about my life from birth to the present, November 2020. I know some sound like fiction, but it is all true. I don't remember everything, and some things I decided not to write about. As you can see, I grew up in the military, so my life is still based around military. I want my children and your children to see what Black citizens have gone through and where we are trying to get to in life—equal rights, that's all. This book is also in memory of my parents, the late Rev. H. A. Hamner Sr. and Mrs. Mary Lou Hamner. I decided to finish with pictures to show where I come from to get to here. Thanks to my friend Larry Brown, who inspired me to keep writing.

Some Pictures of
Pain and Suffering

Edward R. Leon Hamner Sr.

Y ou have read the story of my life in pictures, and it is all true, with real pictures. This book is nonfiction. I still remember them days.

Notes

Edward R. Leon Hamner Sr.

Rev. Edward R. Leon Hamner Sr.
God Bless you and the United States of America

Welcome to the United States of America

About the Author

E dward Hamner Sr. is legally blind. He was born a twin; however, his twin brother was born dead. He is the seventh child of twelve. He was born in Cottondale, Alabama, and raised in Peterson, Alabama, fifteen miles north of Tuscaloosa, Alabama. He grew up in a town with a population of three hundred. There was no type of building, just first-floor homes, no utility for Black people, nowhere to shop, only two grocery stores, and no school for Black children. In 1948, they were able to attend school about twenty miles from where they lived. After high school, he went in the military. After military services, he became a real estate appraiser, paralegal, income tax agency, EMT, and a notary. He is a BMI publisher and a minister (preacher), also a gospel songwriter.

www.ingramcontent.com/pod-product-compliance
Lightning Source LLC
Chambersburg PA
CBHW030307130626
46549CB00002B/732